On My Way
in Planned Giving

About the Author

G. Roger Schoenhals is the editor and publisher of *Planned Giving Today*, a newsletter for charitable gift planners (see below). Before creating the newsletter, Roger served several years as director of the Seattle Pacific Foundation and as the chief planned giving officer for Seattle Pacific University. He has also served as a college teacher and as the editorial director of a Midwest publishing house. He is a graduate of Seattle Pacific University and holds advanced degrees in counseling psychology and theology.

Roger resides in Seattle and provides limited planned giving consulting services for nonprofit organizations and estate planning professionals. He is past president of the Washington Planned Giving Council and serves on various local and national boards.

A prolific writer, Roger has published more than 1,500 articles in numerous periodicals. For several years he provided writing seminars throughout the United States.

He and his wife, Sandra, have four children. Interests include boating, flying float planes and spending several weekends each year as a volunteer ranger in the Alpine Lakes Wilderness Area of the Washington Cascades.

About *Planned Giving Today*

Launched in September 1990, *Planned Giving Today* is an attractive 12-page, 8 1/2-by-11 inch, monthly newsletter written by and for charitable gift planners throughout the United States and Canada. It is known as "The Practical Newsletter for Gift-Planning Professionals" and is read by several thousand nonprofit and for-profit planners. For a complimentary copy and subscription information, call 800-KALL-PGT.

About This Book

The back page of *Planned Giving Today* is the editor's place to pour a cup of coffee and talk shop with his readers. The column is called "On My Way" and includes anecdotes and advice from his personal experience related to planned giving. Several readers have suggested that these vignettes be placed in a single volume. Hence, this book. It contains 88 of the more popular pieces that appeared in "On My Way" during the first five years of publication.

On My Way in Planned Giving

G. Roger Schoenhals

A book by
PLANNED GIVING T·O·D·A·Y®

NOTICE

This book is published and sold with the understanding that neither the publisher nor the author is engaged in rendering legal, accounting or other professional service. If legal advice or other expert assistance is required, the services of a competent professional person should be sought. (From a Declaration of Principles jointly adopted by a Committee of the American Bar Association and a Committee of Publishers.)

Copyright © 1995 by G. Roger Schoenhals
Planned Giving Today
2315 NW 198th Street
Seattle WA 98177
1-800-KALL-PGT

All rights reserved. Except in the case of brief quotations embodied in critical articles and reviews, no part of this publication may be reproduced, stored in a retrieval system, or transmitted in any form or by any means, without the prior permission in writing of the publisher.

ISBN 0-9645517-1-3
Printed in the United States of America

*To Sandy, my wife
and traveling companion
for more than 30 years.*

Contents

	Introduction	11
1.	Whooping It Up on I-5	15
2.	Hearing Aids	16
3.	Shuttle Diplomacy	18
4.	Laughing on the Lawn	19
5.	Take Your Boss	21
6.	Cheerful Givers	22
7.	Ultimate High	23
8.	Inner Circle	24
9.	Be You	26
10.	Dancing With Attorneys	27
11.	Yelling at Norma	29
12.	How to KISS	30
13.	Deep Trouble	31
14.	Lighten Up	32
15.	Breaking Stride	35
16.	Write it Down	36
17.	Those Wild and Crazy Carpet Guys	38
18.	Checklists	39
19.	Dick's Office	40
20.	Helping With Our Ears	42
21.	Recognition Mission	43
22.	Love Those Questions	45
23.	Furnaces and PS	46
24.	Which Attorney?	47
25.	When No Means Yes	48
26.	All Aboard!	49
27.	Leftovers	51
28.	Automated Gratitude	52
29.	Good Timing	53

30.	And the Gift Goes On	54
31.	The Low Road	55
32.	The High Road	55
33.	Bitten by the Bug	56
34.	Partial to Print	58
35.	Artful Juxtaposition	59
36.	A Few Resolutions	59
37.	Three More Resolutions	60
38.	A Pause That Refreshes	61
39.	Looking Good	62
40.	Birthday Party Madness	62
41.	The Annuity Connection	63
42.	The Second Mile	65
43.	Gift Planner's Dilemma	67
44.	Flinging the Seed	68
45.	When PGOs Cry	69
46.	Shortsighted Savings	70
47.	Stair Peak	71
48.	Drip, Drip	73
49.	Gratification and Character	75
50.	Such a Great Profession	76
51.	Deferred Recognition	77
52.	Bring the Kids Along	78
53.	The Enriching Effect of Planned Giving	79
54.	The Puzzle	80
55.	Try TRUST	82
56.	Where to Put Anger	83
57.	Surprises at the Door	84
58.	Serendipity Gifts	85
59.	All-Day Suckers	86
60.	Today!	88
61.	The Receipt Connection	89

62.	Just Horsin' Around	90
63.	The Big Picture	92
64.	Name Dropping	93
65.	On Rearing Philanthropists	94
66.	Take This Outline, Please	95
67.	Trusts and Trust	96
68.	Setting the Tone	97
69.	Planned Giving at Home	98
70.	Good Intentions	99
71.	Appetizing Alternatives	101
72.	Procedures, Procedures	103
73.	A Little Help From Our Friends	105
74.	When Gift Planners Collide	106
75.	Hourly Professionals	107
76.	Out of the Blue	108
77.	Charitable Hints	109
78.	Think Zoo	110
79.	Jokes Attorneys Tell	111
80.	Living 200 Years	113
81.	Self-Improvement	114
82.	Going for It	115
83.	Seminar in a Cookie	117
84.	Practicing With Each Other	118
85.	Table Hopping	118
86.	The Personal Touch	119
87.	Segment of One	120
88.	A Piece of the Action	121
Postscript		123

Introduction

Pooled income funds had something to do with swimming. Gift annuities involved Christmas. And charitable *remainder* unitrusts reminded me of division problems in math class. And furthermore, the term "planned gibbing" sounded a bit fishy to me.

So I was mystified when the executive vice president from my alma mater asked me to apply for a planned giving position. He said, "We're looking for a person to head our new foundation and to run our planned giving program . . . and we think you're just the one for the job."

Running a foundation? Planned giving? I knew zilch about one and zero about the other. But since I was getting weary of eking out a living as a freelance writer, I decided to apply.

So I updated my resume and filled out the application form. A week later I stepped onto campus and began a six-hour interview process that took me to several offices. At 4:00 p.m. I ended where I began, sitting across the desk from the vice president for university advancement.

I said, "I appreciate your confidence in me, but I just don't think I'm the right person for this job. It's completely over my head. You need someone more qualified."

We parted amiably.

Four months later I was again invited to come to campus for an interview. They had failed to find the "right" person and wanted me to reconsider.

This time we all met together in one room — three vice presidents and two or three other top officials. They talked about my long history with the university (growing up on campus as a faculty kid) and my service and reputation in related organizations.

They spoke of their concern to find someone who understood the mission of the school, who knew many of the older alumni and who demonstrated skill in interpersonal relationships. "We think a half-way intelligent person can gain the technical skills, but when it comes to relational skills — you either have them or you don't. We want somebody who cares about people and who will represent this place with integrity. We want someone who can help others to invest in the future of this place."

I looked behind me to see who they were talking to.

By the time I left that office, I was invigorated, not only because of their words of affirmation and the confidence they expressed in me, but because they had sparked a vision in me of a new vocation and a grand opportunity to make a significant difference in the future of my alma mater.

I began October 1, 1986. And from that day, I have tried to emphasize the relational skills that can make or break a planned giving officer.

Planned giving, I believe, is the process of inspiring and enabling persons to make tax-wise gifts that will benefit them inwardly as well as materially and that will further result in helping a worthy organization advance its mission in the world.

Gift planning is a people-centered profession. It is people who care about our organizations. People make the gifts. People pass along the good news. It's people, people, people.

Consequently, when I launched *Planned Giving Today* in 1990, I wanted to provide a publication that would dwell on the practical aspects of planned giving — the people-related things. And so we dubbed it, "The Practical Newsletter for Gift-Planning Professionals."

Further, I wanted to write a column that contained person-to-person, shop-talk kind of material that would remind all of us of the human side of our profession. My own experience had taught me how easy it is to become technically transfixed, to love proposals more than people.

The back page column, "On My Way," was and is my way of underscoring the personal element in planned giving. Sometimes this column is a soap box for me to express my convictions. Sometimes it's a sand box to play in. And sometimes it's a lunch box where I tuck a tasty treat for the reader to take along the way.

Always, it's a batter's box where I stand at the plate and swing.

Sometimes I strike out (groan). Occasionally, I hit a single or double (grin). And once in a great while I smack it over the fence (glee).

This book is a collection of my base hits and home runs, at least from my perspective. You may see it differently from where you sit. A fly ball drifting into foul territory. An infield grounder followed by a side-arm snap from the short stop beating me out at first base — "He's Out!"

I've presented the 88 "articlettes" in mostly random order, but with some attention to variation of length and subject matter. In a few places I adjusted the text to eliminate or alter time-sensitive or otherwise inappropriate references. Still, 99 percent of the text is exactly the way it originally appeared in the newsletter.

The subtitle of this book indicates that I have aimed my word processor at planned giving officers and others involved in charitable gift planning. There is, however, value in these pages for anyone serving in the development community -- development directors, annual fund promoters, major gift solicitors, special event coordinators, etc. If nothing else, these vignettes can create understanding and appreciation for what those of us in planned giving actually do.

When a board member or family member or a professional advisor or a donor or even the person sitting next to you on the plane asks, "What kind of work do you do?" you no longer have to confound them with oratorical contortions extolling the fine art of deferred giving and the awesome benefits of a net-income charitable remainder unitrust with make-up provision. Nor must you launch a 60-second crash course on the peculiarities, challenges and rewards of your esoteric work. Now you can simply hand them this book and say, "Here, read this."

Finally, my earnest hope is that the following anecdotes and advice will make your travels more productive as you continue *on your way* in planned giving.

— GRS

1
Whooping It Up on I-5

Blessed are the donors who make gift planning fun. I'm thinking particularly of the Nelsons. When I left their house the other day I smiled all the way home — all 60 miles.

As soon as I hit the I-5 freeway, I called my wife on the car phone. "San, I just had the most wonderful visit with the Nelsons. They are pure joy. I've never had a gift go so well. You've gotta meet them."

All the way home I thought about the Nelsons and why they were bringing me such enjoyment. I thought about the way they let me into their lives. Though I was a new friend to them, they opened their finances to me — their assets and liabilities, their concerns for retirement needs and contingency planning.

They told me about their family. They wanted me to understand the interpersonal dynamics and why they were giving this gift instead of passing it along to the kids. They confided in me.

They related their involvement with the charity and what they wanted to accomplish. They spoke of an "enduring gift" that would continue to give after they are gone, an endowment to benefit the less fortunate.

As I drove along thinking about the Nelsons, I could no longer contain myself. I tell you the truth when I say I smacked the top of the steering wheel with my hand and let out a whoop. (The silence that followed seemed a bit eerie.)

I thought about the afternoon Mr. Nelson took me to see the property. We got out of the car and walked through the grassy lot. It is a marvelous piece of real estate, commercially zoned in a growing area of town. He told me about the developers in the wings who were drooling over the property. As we walked, he gestured where he saw a building sitting and where the parking area might be. His voice and animated manner expressed excitement over the property and the gift they would soon make.

Along with their acceptance and openness, the Nelsons expressed trust in me as a professional and as the representative of the charity. "We won't do anything without checking with you first," Mr. Nelson said. "I want you to be in the center of this whole process."

He arranged for me to meet their accountant to discuss the workings of the charitable remainder unitrust. He wanted me to look over their will and other papers. He wanted me to make sure his wife understood the gift plan frontwards and backwards. He asked that I be available to their attorney. The confidence they expressed in me made me feel 10 feet tall.

Not only did they invite me into their lives and demonstrate trust in me, they honored me with their friendship and gratitude. Each time they greeted me with enthusiasm and walked me to the car when I left. They made me feel valued. They looked to me as the one who would help them give their "ultimate gift."

By the time I arrived home and eased the car into the garage, I was pumped up for another 20 years in gift planning. It just doesn't get any better.

2
Hearing Aids

"Dad, you should get a hearing aid." That little statement, delivered by my 14-year-old daughter while tooling down the Interstate on a family vacation, evoked a 10-minute discourse during which I earnestly set forth an impressive list of infallible proofs on my excellent ear power.

But try as I might to denounce it, I've had to admit that my family (and doctor) are right about me inching closer to the ranks of the audibly challenged. Could it actually be that someday I will need the assistance of a hearing aid? (Hmmmmm . . . come to think of it, I should have my eyesight checked again.)

You'll understand, now, why I perked up when the speaker announced he would be talking about hearing aids. I quickly discovered, however, that his presentation was not about little gizmos in the ear. He orated on the importance of active listening and provided a list of aids to help us toward that goal.

And since a good part of our success as gift planners depends on our ability to hear the spoken and unspoken messages of our donors, I thought you'd find a few of these aids worthwhile.

First, listen with your eyes. Observe the person carefully. Remember, 80 percent of communication is nonverbal. Look at posture. Note facial expressions and gestures. Does the person offer you coffee while glancing at a clock? This is *saying* one thing and *showing* you another.

In my graduate work in counseling psychology, we videotaped our counseling sessions. Each of us then studied a session using a monitor without audio. Laboriously, we wrote detailed descriptions, including measurements, of everything the counselee did during the session. We were amazed to see how much we could actually learn about the person by simply examining appearance, expression and behavior.

Look, too, at the person's environment. You can "hear" a lot from furniture, pictures, books and magazines, the degree of cleanliness and other "voices" in the room.

Learn to listen optically.

Second, listen with your heart. Enter into the conversation with an empathetic spirit. Feel the emotions displayed in tone of voice, volume, pitch, inflections, speed of speech, emotion-laden statements and other audible clues. Hearing well at this level can provide a window to the person's true inner feelings.

For example, if the person sounds lethargic, you may discover the presence of grief. Or if the person speaks loudly and hurriedly, you may divine they are under some kind of personal stress. Of course, it could also mean they are late for an appointment to get a hearing aid!

Third, listen with your time. Certainly, there is a place for pop-in/pop-out visits. But more often than not, many of us will have to admit we want to move on to the next visit if the person seems at all disinterested. After all, we have to make our quota.

By giving the donor our time, by letting them ramble on, we can often unlock information that will help us target our appeal. Unhurried listening is hard work and takes patience. It costs time, but pays dividends.

So there you have it: eyes, heart, time — three hearing aids to make us better listeners. Take them along on your next visit.

3
Shuttle Diplomacy

Some gifts require a Henry Kissinger kind of diplomacy. First you cultivate the donor and work through difficulties that might impede a gift (i.e., mortgaged property). Then you go to your organization and "negotiate" the acceptance of the out-of-the-ordinary gift. Then back to the donors to refine their gift proposal.

Then back to the gift acceptance committee. Then back to the donors for further adjustments . . . and assurances that the charity really does want their gift. Then back to the charity with positive words about the donors' intent and the benefits of accepting the gift. Back and forth you go, diplomatically bringing together the giver and the receiver, keeping spirits high.

And when you step aside to collect your thoughts, you reflect on the fact that nowhere in your training did you receive any direction on shuttle diplomacy. You never attended a seminar or read a book about it. Still, it's part of your job. And when those delicate times come, you rise to the challenge . . . because if you don't, the donor loses heart, the gift falls through and the charity gets upset. You do it because you're a one-in-a-million kind of person — a planned giving professional.

4
Laughing on the Lawn

My first glimpse of the competition unnerves me — a multitude of sleek bodies representing nearly every age. From the safety of the car, I scan the scene, hoping to find at least one specimen in worse shape than me. No luck.

I turn to my wife in horror. She gives me an understanding look. The kids jabber away, "Win the race, Daddy. Win the race, Daddy."

I open the door slowly and step into the sweltering heat. It must be 100 degrees and the humidity even more.

Bidding farewell to my little family, I walk tentatively toward the runners. I feel every eye beholding my new shoes, new socks, new shorts, new shirt.

Panicky thoughts race through my mind as I maneuver through the cross country teams, veteran running stars, out-of-town marathon junkies and spirited young people bouncing up and down eager to begin.

I sign in at the card table and receive a number. My hands tremble as I pin it to my shirt.

My first foot race. I begin to wish I had done more jogging to prepare. I wish I had lost 30 pounds. I wish . . .

But it was only a week ago that I decided to run in this annual two-mile race celebrating the founding of Warsaw, Indiana.

Some of the runners do stretches and calisthenics on the grass. Others sprint up and down the road. I stand perfectly still, not wanting to waste one iota of energy.

I notice an ambulance nearby. It will follow us, I learn, to pick up any casualties. The thought consoles me.

Time to line up. We bunch together ready for the gun to sound. I squeeze in at the front. At least I'll be in the lead for part of the race.

The course will take us one block west, one block south, and then we'll turn left for the long run into the middle of town where the crowds wait. Another series of left turns will bring us to the finish line at the courthouse square.

Bang! I lurch forward. Seconds later I'm looking at 95 percent of the runners moving out in front of me. Reaching the first corner I start my turn and catch a glimpse of the pack disappearing around the next corner. It's the last I see of them.

I wonder what pace I can run and still finish. Perhaps I'm going too slow. I speed up. No, that's too fast. I slow down.

A panting sound behind me brings hope. At least I'm not last. I determine to keep ahead of that noise.

Gasping and swimming in sweat, I reach the halfway mark. My body is calling me names. I think about the ambulance. A side alley looks inviting.

But I press on, pushed by the heavy panting behind.

Just then I hear a question measured out in great gasps of agony. "Why," my pursuer asks, "are we doing this?"

The question plagues me the rest of the race. I sift through a list of reasons. None of them ring a bell. But still I run on.

I pass clowns and floats and marching units waiting to begin the parade which follows the race. Yogi the Bear dances alongside me for a few yards. Not funny.

Now I can see people lining the curbs leaning out, looking down the road, straining to see who the final runners are. Salt runs into my eyes. It burns.

Just when I need it most I hear a little voice calling, "Daddy, Daddy." I glance to the left and see my two preschoolers waving wildly. Mommy oozes with empathy.

Six blocks to go. A runner in front of me slows his pace. The gap closes and I come beside him. I sputter an encouraging word. He mumbles something about going up a hill. (It's flat.)

We round two corners and head for the courthouse. All I can see through the blur is a mass of people. It motivates me. I floor the accelerator. Nothing happens.

Finally I see the finish line pass under my feet. I gasp wildly for air. My knees buckle.

A nice Red Cross lady takes my arm and hands me a cup of

cold juice. I stagger to a shady spot on the courthouse lawn. I collapse and begin to giggle . . . then laugh . . . then guffaw. It was good to be in the race and better to finish.

Sometimes, in planned giving work, you may question why you run so hard. You may feel unprepared and inadequate to accomplish your goals. You may want desperately to throw in the towel. The grass looks greener down a side street.

But staying in the race, keeping on when you feel like quitting, is what perseverance is all about. If you stay with it long enough, you'll find a measure of success. You'll cross your own finish lines and have reason to roll on the grass and laugh.

5
Take Your Boss

A few times in my career as a planned giving officer of a university, I was able to get the president to go with me on a prospect call. Before the appointment, I made sure he had a "fact sheet" about the prospect(s) and knew what I expected of him during the visit. I took pains to involve him only in appropriate calls and to prearrange the visit with the prospect.

On the appointment day, I picked up the president (on time) and drove him to the prospect's home. We reviewed the background information during the ride. Once there, I introduced the president and allowed him to interact with the prospect and to report on the organization, its mission, its needs and his dreams for the future. And to challenge the prospect to deepen his or her support.

Rather than lay out a specific gift proposal, we viewed the time as advanced cultivation. The specific appeal came later during a follow-up contact when the prospect and I reviewed the president's visit and the needs of the institution.

Having the president come for a visit always proved valuable.

It was a highlight for the prospect and, I think, a benefit to the president. It gave him a chance to meet with a good friend of the institution and permitted him to share his plans and concerns in person. He always seemed to come away from the visit energized by the contact with a supporter. It also made my work easier by elevating my role as a representative of the president in the prospect's eyes.

I enjoyed these times of getting to know the president on a personal level. I absorbed his heartbeat for the institution and was better able to communicate it to others. I also felt he had a better understanding of my work.

If I were back at the university, I'd sit down with the president's secretary and try to carve out of his schedule one afternoon a month. Then I would focus my efforts on arranging visits with the "cream of my contacts." I would aim to make this time the high point of the president's month.

6
Cheerful Givers

People who give well are good to be around. Not only for the sake of receiving a gift, but to benefit from the quality of their lives. Their giving reflects a generous, supportive attitude. They care about the organization and its mission. They enjoy giving their gifts. What a lift they provide!

I think of a retired faculty member. He and his spouse used an appreciated asset to meet some of their charitable goals. The day he delivered the gift he was grinning from ear to ear. I thought, *This man is having the time of his life.*

I think of another couple who used a piece of real estate to establish a charitable trust. As a pastoral team they had earned little in the way of money. But time and good stewardship produced an asset which enabled them to make a significant gift.

The pleasure they found in making the gift enriched my life. I think of a widow who spent days cautiously considering a planned gift. No smiles, just thoughtful deliberation. But once she signed the documents her demeanor changed. Convinced she had made a wise choice, she relaxed and beamed satisfaction. Even today, years later, she expresses happiness about her gift.

Other givers come to mind. And in every case I see glowing faces. I find ample evidence that it is indeed "more blessed to give than to receive."

7
Ultimate High

A few weeks ago, on the weekend, I received a phone call from a person I had helped to establish a two-life charitable remainder unitrust with previously encumbered property. Bill had maneuvered around the encumbrance problems by obtaining a "bridge loan" to pay off the existing mortgage. After the appropriate legal work, he deeded two/thirds of the property to the trust and retained the other third for himself. Then he and the trustees sold the property together and each received their share. Bill used his third to pay off his loan and the trustees took their share and invested it to meet the terms of the trust.

Back to the phone call. Bill simply wanted to thank me for my part in the process. It had taken several years and lots of visits to bring this gift about, but once it happened, he was thrilled. And he wanted me to know. Even though both he and his wife, Joanne, had expressed this several times before, he called to say it again.

It reminded me of another couple I had helped a few months earlier with a charitable remainder unitrust that also involved a piece of debt-encumbered real estate. Again, it took a while to work things out, but they finally achieved their goal of making a substantial deferred gift to several charities while caring for their current retirement needs.

One evening, with the signed documents and some other materials in hand, I drove out to their home several miles east of Seattle. It was 7:00 p.m. and they knew I was coming from the office.

I arrived to find the table set. Walter and Donna accepted no excuses and sat me down for dinner. As we shared the meal, they repeatedly expressed their excitement over their trust and about my help. They couldn't thank me enough. They wanted to know what they could do to "get the word out."

Anyone who's been involved as a gift planner for very long knows exactly what I'm talking about here. Folks like Bill and Joanne and Walter and Donna make it all worthwhile. They fall over us with gratitude for a gift well planned, and we feel great. It's the ultimate high.

8
Inner Circle

A knock at the front door interrupted my slippage into sleep. As I reached for my clothes, I noted the time: 10:00 P.M. *Now who could that be?* I wondered.

My 13-year-old raced to the door and called out, "Who is it?" The muffled response was interpreted a moment later as she entered my room and announced the name of our visitor. For this article, I'll call him Tom.

Why would he be coming here to see me . . . and at this hour? It's been two years.

I opened the door and exchanged greetings. He said he just wanted to stop by and chat for a few minutes. "Come into the kitchen," I said. "We'll sit at the table. Can I fix you something? Some coffee? Tea?"

Tom wore a cap. I noticed his neck was swollen.

He told me of his odyssey with blood-related cancer and the effect it was having on his lymph nodes. He described how the monthly treatments knocked him for a loop. And how he had lost his hair. He said he was going onto disability soon and that the prognosis for beating this thing was zero.

The reason he stopped by was to tell me how he had come to terms with the disease and that he had reordered his priorities. "I know it sounds funny," he said, "but I am more alive today than ever." He spoke of a religious awakening and how he was seeking to make the most out of every day. He just wanted me to know these things.

He talked about his children and his wife. He told me about work and his circle of friends and the awkwardness of relating to some of them.

An hour and a half later, he left. I climbed back into bed and grasped again for sleep. Repeatedly, it slipped through my fingers.

I thought of my earlier visits with Tom and our conversations about his gift and estate plan. He had wanted to make sure everything was done well — all the bases covered, including a good attorney. There had been no hint of cancer.

Tom's appearance at my door reminded me of the life-and-death issues relating to the gift and estate planning process. Our work takes us into the lives of people where we touch matters of ultimate concern — values, family, death, life's treasures, immortality.

This is one of the unique features of the planned giving profession. We are allowed special privileges by those who trust us and the organizations we represent. We become part of their inner circle. And when the foundations of life are shaken, sometimes we're called upon to offer a gift of time — time for listening, time for caring, time for speaking words of consolation and encouragement.

Planned giving is so much more than extracting a gift.

9
Be You

The hour-long program featured three speakers, each one a notable success in building a productive planned giving program. The first speaker delivered a dynamic talk about his promotional activities and the great visibility his program had in the community. Type A personality. Madison Avenue.

The second speaker changed the pace and spoke with softer tones. He emphasized the critical importance of building a program on relational skills. "The key to successful gift planning," he said, "is to find out what people need and then to meet those needs." He used the term "caring" numerous times.

Speaker three touted the technical. A CPA, he relished the nuts and bolts of gift planning and talked about his success in working with professional advisors in his city. "I'm a resource to the estate planning community when it comes to planned giving," he said. "Our biggest gifts come from the advisors I've networked with over the past seven years."

Three speakers, three different approaches, three successful programs.

Sometimes I think we try to squeeze every planned giving officer into a single mold. "If you want to succeed, you've got to _____." But, in fact, there are several ways to succeed in planned giving. The key is to find where your strengths lie and then to build on those strengths.

If you're gifted as a promoter, build on that strength. If you have a special sensitivity to people and the ability to get close to them, lead with that trait. If you thrive on the technical aspects of planned giving, let that be your forte.

But remember, your greatest strength can also be your greatest weakness. The aggressive gift planner can get on people's nerves. The people person can have warm and fuzzy friendships that rarely produce a gift. The technician can lose touch with common people.

So keep your perspective. Work on those areas where you are weak. Be kindhearted to those around you with other strengths. Finally, in conclusion and lastly — and I say this as I step down from my soap box — whatever your strengths are, find them and go with them. Be yourself. Enjoy yourself. Don't let others around you squeeze you into their mold.

10
Dancing With Attorneys

This is a true story. It happened. Trust me. A few years ago, on December 15, an attorney from a town in southwestern Washington state (attorney A) called me and said he had a client who wanted to establish a charitable remainder unitrust with the university's foundation before the end of the year. He didn't know much about "those things" so he asked me to send him some information.

I ran off a full-blown proposal using my handy-dandy planned giving software. The materials included a sample unitrust agreement and a thorough analysis. I also stuck into the package a sample agreement we had used several times, drafted by an estate planning attorney who was a friend of the university (attorney B). This sample agreement was shorter than the one produced by the software. Sending two different sample agreements proved to be a major mistake.

Attorney A reviewed the two documents and then shipped a copy of each one to an estate planning attorney who practiced law in a town north of Seattle (attorney C). This attorney was probating the estate of a close relative of attorney A's client. Money from this estate was coming to the client and would be used to fund the trust. (Are you with me?)

Attorney A told me he liked the *shorter* version and asked that I have attorney B draft a document using his format and wording.

In the meantime, attorney A received input from attorney C which involved a merging of the two sample documents. The merged document favored the *longer* version.

A few days later I rushed the document prepared by attorney B to attorney A. Instead of using this document, he went to work drafting a "final" document using the merged document from attorney C and the newly created document from attorney B. (Still with me?)

Time was running out. I asked attorney A to fax a copy of his new document to the chairman of our gifts acceptance committee in Seattle who was, himself, an attorney (attorney D) for his review. Attorney A did so and also faxed a copy to the creative lawyer north of Seattle, attorney C.

I met attorney D at his office where we went through the faxed document. I had with me a copy of the computer-generated sample agreement produced by the software creator who is also an attorney (attorney E). I also had a copy of the new document prepared by attorney B (at the request of attorney A). As we went through the new document prepared by attorney A and tried to compare it with the original documents produced by attorneys B and E, we found ourselves babbling incoherently.

Finally, attorney D concluded that the hybrid document produced by attorney A met the foundation's criteria and that the six-figure cash gift was certainly acceptable. Elated that we could now proceed with the gift, I called attorney A with the news. Meanwhile, attorney A had heard from attorney C saying she wanted to go through the document with more detail and that she would fax him a fresh copy the next morning, December 30. (Reliving this is killing me!)

Attorney C did, in fact, find some things to change. So after getting her changes, Attorney A drafted a final version. He read me the changes over the phone: nothing that would keep the foundation from managing the trust. So I said, "Let's go for it."

I drove down Interstate 5 to a restaurant south of Tacoma. At the same time, the donor, with the freshly prepared documents and a cashier's check, drove north to meet me. Two men on a mission. Two cars rushing to an appointed place on the last day of the year. (Is this adventure or what?)

I arrived first and took a seat. After ten minutes I ordered coffee. Then lunch. Then dessert and coffee. Then more coffee. Finally, a man entered the restaurant carrying a package. We had never met and I peered at him inquisitively. He looked around for a planned giving officer. And then he saw me and he knew.

He joined me at the table and we talked. He ordered lunch and I ordered more coffee. I learned about his interest in the university and why he was making this deferred gift. Finally, he placed into my trembling hands (too much caffeine) the signed documents and a humongous check. I thanked him profusely.

We walked to the parking lot, climbed into our respective cars and headed home. Mission accomplished. December 31.

11
Yelling at Norma

Ninety-nine-year-old Norma lived on the eighth floor of a retirement home here in Seattle. On a wintery afternoon, I dropped by to see her. I checked in at the front desk and asked if they'd call her to see whether I could come up for a short visit and to deliver a poinsettia.

The attendant let the phone ring and ring. No answer. "I know she's there," the lady said. "She's probably not wearing her hearing aid. Why don't you just go up and knock?"

Getting off the elevator, I headed down the long hall to her room. The carpet led directly to her door.

I could hear the television or radio behind the door so I knocked briskly. After a pause, I repeated my knock, this time a bit stronger. Again, no response. The next series of knocks shook the door and reverberated down the hall. I half expected *every* door to open and a riot to ensue. Surprisingly, nothing.

I was ready to pound the door with both fists when I heard a raspy voice. "Who is it?"

"It's Roger Schoenhals from Seattle Pacific University," I said. "I have a Christmas plant for you."

"Who is it?" she asked again.

I repeated myself loudly.

Again, "Who is it?"

I yelled.

A door opened behind me and a nice little lady said, "She can't hear you. Why don't you just leave the plant by the door? I'll see her at dinner and tell her you were here. She'll have her hearing aid on then."

I jotted a note on my business card and stuck it in the plant. Then I headed for the elevator.

Driving off to my next visit, I thought about Norma. *How come she didn't put on her hearing aid when she knew someone was at the door? Why didn't she just open the door to see who was there? Did I yell loud enough?*

Another unsolved mystery in the life of a planned giving officer.

12
How to KISS

"Keep it Simple Stupid" is a rather crass reminder that we gift planners must continually struggle to take the complex and make it understandable to our donor prospects. The best way to do this is to first thoroughly understand what we are trying to relate. Two quotes come to mind:

William Jennings Bryan wrote, "You cannot make people understand a subject unless you understand that subject yourself."

C. S. Lewis put it this way, "I have come to the conviction that if you cannot translate your thoughts into uneducated language, then your thoughts were confused. Power to translate is the test of having really understood one's own meaning."

A further aid to clear communication is to corral a couple of young teens and explain a planned gift arrangement until they are able to repeat it back. The problem here is keeping them in the corral long enough to hear your message.

One more suggestion. Write out your thoughts and then read them aloud. The writing part will force you to think through the ideas as you formulate coherent sentences. The reading part will allow you to hear the flow of words and any awkward transitions. Finally, put on your editor's cap and reduce multisyllabic words and long sentences. This will take time, of course, but the process will help you "Keep it Short and Sweet."

13
Deep Trouble

The phone rang and the real estate broker introduced himself. "I have a client," he said, "who wants to give you a piece of land in exchange for one of those unitrusts. If you have a minute, I'd like to take you over to see it. It's only a mile or two away."

"Yes, yes, let's do it; I'll be out in front waiting."

The excitement mounted as I waited. *This is my lucky day!*

In the car I quizzed him about the property. I asked about the donor, about any ties he had with the university, about the reasons for his proposed gift. I understand now why his answers were fuzzy, incomplete.

We turned down a lane and then into a clearing. And then the road simply dropped out of sight. I walked over to the edge and looked down into a deep gully littered with garbage. Dumbfounded, I asked where the property lines ran. He said basically from where we stood to the rim on the other side. In other words, nothing on top, everything in the gully. My mouth dropped open as wide as the hole in front of me.

I made my way down the steep bank, wanting to check out the pool of water down there. It was deep and rancid. Looking up the gully I could see a giant sewer pipe crossing the gap on a trestle. Something was seeping out midspan, splashing into a little stream that ran down the center of the gully. Gross.

I glanced up and saw the realtor watching me. I thought, *I can't believe this. Who does this man think I am? How can he possibly think we'd be interested in this property?*

As I climbed out of there, my temperature rose. He seemed a bit uncomfortable as I approached. "This is an environmental nightmare," I said. "It will never fly as a gift. Has it been on the market at all? Have you tried to sell it?"

He came clean. The owner had indeed tried to sell it, repeatedly. Even tried to give it away. But he thought just maybe we might be interested.

The salesman began to apologize: "I told him you wouldn't want it, but he wanted me to try anyway. I certainly understand your position."

This happened three years ago and I'm still shaking my head. It stands in my mind as a reminder that not all gifts are noble. Some are white elephants. Some are holes in the ground. Always look before you leap.

14

Lighten Up

This morning I called the planned giving office of a local charity. I made the mistake of asking the person on the other end of the line, "How are things going?"

"Not so good. I just can't seem to keep up with things. Sometimes I wonder whether I'm in the right job."

Doing planned giving can take its toll. You have endless committee meetings, unfinished tasks, pressures to perform well, the fear of technical incompetence, and more donors and prospects than you can possibly visit. It all adds up to Excedrin headache number 79.

But instead of a pill, reach for a bit of humor. Lean back in your chair and visualize your circumstance as a cartoonist might depict it. How would he or she draw your discouraged countenance? Can you squeeze out a smile as you think about this? If you can, you may just find the added lift to go on with your work.

Most of us need a good chuckle now and then to keep us sane. We need to learn how to laugh at ourselves and to see the humor in difficult situations.

Wholesome humor eases tension, promotes health, encourages good will and helps us cope with life. A good belly laugh does wonders for both body and soul.

Of course, inappropriate humor can have a detrimental affect. No one truly benefits when we make others the butt of our jokes, when we use poor taste in humor or when we crack one-liners at the wrong time. While some people may err in using humor wrongfully, most of us probably err in not using good humor enough.

Some good, old-fashioned fun in the workplace can lighten the atmosphere and help everyone perform their work a little more cheerfully. For example, the director of development and I had a running game with a 2-inch by 10-inch plastic sign titled, "No Soliciting." I'd find it in the weirdest places — computer screen, desk drawer, inside coat pocket. Once I found it taped to my office ceiling.

It became a challenge to our creativity to deliver the sign back to the other person in an unexpected way. One time I mailed it to him from some distant location, with a silly return name and address. Once I put the sign in a place where it went undiscovered for so long I had to rehide it just to keep the "ping-pong game" going.

Back and forth the little sign went, with just enough interlude to create suspense. Not overdoing a good thing. Not letting it get out of hand. But a little ongoing playfulness that produced a smile or two in the office.

A dumb thing to do? Immature? Undignified? Yeah, probably all those things. But fun. And, alas, one of the things I miss since leaving that office several years ago.

Do you need to lighten up a little? How about picking out a series of humorous cards and mailing them to members of your office staff over a period of several weeks? Disguise your handwriting and sign the name of a fictitious person. You'll create a stir and eventually become the target of suspicion since you're the only one not receiving a card. By the way, the more unlikely you are to do something like this, the more fun it will be when they finally discover that you, of all people, did it.

Occasionally, when you find a good cartoon, label it and send it to a colleague. You'll both have a good laugh. I've had some great fun with Far Side creations.

If you possess the art of discernment, you might even try a practical joke or two. One of my friends went to his office and found it entirely empty. Funny, in a way, but I'd steer away from such monumental efforts. Keep things simple.

Humor is a tricky thing. Sometimes a little goes a long way. You don't want to dish it out recklessly. Nor do you want to be known as the resident prankster.

Appropriate humor is an endearing quality. Some of the people I like best are good-natured folk who wear a smile and laugh easily. I want to be more like that.

Three cheers for cheerfulness! It's a virtue to be pursued. A mental attitude to embrace. A means to more gifts.

More gifts? Well, I can't prove it, of course. But I believe it. It just seems to me that a friendly smile and a good sense of humor contributes more to gift-giving than a billion brain cells crammed with technical understanding and stored behind a sourpuss face.

But it doesn't have to be technical knowledge *or* a sense of humor. We can have both! That's one reason I think so highly of Conrad Teitell — he's a technician's technician, but he also has a mile-long funny bone.

So lighten up. Put a little fun in your work.

15

Breaking Stride

I padded down the country road at a sluggish pace. It was a hot day to be jogging 12 miles. I had never run that far before. But when I passed the 10-mile mark I decided to push on and reach for the big 12.

My feet hurt. My legs weighed 300 pounds. My lungs ached.

As I moved into the final mile I watched an approaching car slow down. The passenger lowered her window.

"Pardon me," she called. "Could you tell us where . . ."

"I can't stop," I sputtered. And ran on.

Had they been going in my direction, moving along beside me while I ran, I would have helped gladly. But, no, they wanted me to stop, to break stride.

It frustrated me. Couldn't they see I was pouring out my sweat to get somewhere? Didn't they know that you never, never interrupt a runner?

I made my 12-mile goal standing up. But the accomplishment tasted sour. I kept thinking of the people in the car and my refusal to stop.

It's easy to chase achievement, to be goal-oriented. "Don't bother me; I want to get this done before lunch." "Can't talk now; I'm in a hurry." "Let's make it some other time; I'm too busy this week."

Obsession with reaching our finish lines produces an inflexible pace. Earnestly we pad down the road, panting out words to those who seek our attention: "I can't stop. I can't talk. I can't help. I can't . . . ."

Many goals are worthy. And establishing and maintaining momentum is important. But the good can be twisted. Programs and projects can keep us from people.

My 12-mile run occurred many years and pounds ago. More recently, while jogging, I had a similar experience with another person seeking information. Again, the car approached and the window went down.

"I'm sorry to bother you," the woman said, "but can you tell me where . . ."

I stopped. And though the answer to her question was clearly visible on a sign 30 feet away, I took the time to provide directions.

Later, when I finished my run, I felt refreshed and good about myself. I think it had something to do with breaking stride.

16
Write it Down

One of the important reminders hammered home last month at the Washington Planned Giving Council annual conference was the value of keeping good records. The speaker, an attorney, made the point repeatedly: "Always write down the gist of personal conversations and keep copies of all correspondence. Maintain a thorough file on each donor. The day will come when you won't regret it."

That day has come for me on several occasions. One episode is a situation where the donor "woke up" after the trust was established and decided it was not really what she wanted.

The planning process had stretched over two years and there had been numerous meetings, including sit-down sessions with her CPA. With full agreement all around, our legal counsel produced trust and transfer documents for the donor.

Duty bound, we insisted that she review this document with

her own independent legal counsel before establishing the trust. Following our promptings, she acquired a lawyer who had been recommended by her financial counselor.

Before we knew it, several changes were made, new documents were drawn and the donor was ready to sign, relieved that "all this legal stuff" was over. We decided to go ahead and accept the trust since the particulars fell within our parameters and the donor appeared to be happy.

Six months later the donor discovered that the payout provisions were not what she had really wanted . . . and not what we had originally discussed. When the donor revisited her attorney to complain, he shifted the blame to the charity (and me), purporting that we had failed to properly inform the donor about the ramifications of the revised gift plan — even though he was the one who advised her to switch the payout provisions and created a document to that effect.

How sweet it was to be able to haul out a file full of notes and records which clearly indicated due diligence on our part. How sweet it was to lay all the allegations and misunderstandings to rest and to regain the confidence of the donor. How bittersweet to see the independent attorney confess to a sloppy job of serving his client. (We were later able to reform the trust.)

Keeping detailed notes of the cultivation and planning process, and writing letters to reinforce what has been said in person may seem tedious and unnecessary, but believe me, nothing can be finer than finding a bulging file of facts when you need them.

After-gift problems can arise because older donors often have fading memories; they may forget conversations and earlier decisions. And sometimes a new (and uninformed) professional advisor can enter the picture and stir up a hornet's nest.

Problems can also evolve when family members learn of the gift and become disgruntled, or even accusatory (i.e., "You talked my mother into doing something she really didn't want to do.").

These kinds of problems pop up when you least expect them. For your sake, for the sake of your organization and for the well-being of your donors, keep good records. Write it down!

17
Those Wild and Crazy Carpet Guys

We needed carpet for Julie's room, so we followed a tip and went to a place called "Four Day Carpet." The name, we discovered, has nothing to do with the age of the rugs, but with the fact that the store is open only four days a week.

When we arrived, we found three or four young, energetic and entrepreneurial fellows leading customers through the stacks of carpet, joking and having a good time. It was drizzling outside, but here in this old warehouse the atmosphere was bright and friendly.

"Have a cup of coffee," the eager salesman said, coming out of nowhere. "What can I do for ya?"

I explained our mission and then fell in behind him, my daughter and wife as we began the yes-no-yes-no-no-yes-yes-no-yes process of selecting just the right carpet for our 13-year-old. An hour later I said, "Hope you're not too frustrated with us."

He replied, "Hey, I'm not a carpet salesman; I'm a customer service attendant. Service is my middle name. Take as long as you want." He then embarked on this marvelous discourse of how they were dedicated to putting the customer first. He told us about the books they were reading and then he said it again, "I'm in service, not sales."

My attention shifted as one of the guys nearby dribbled a basketball and took a shot at a hoop attached to an overhead beam. "You guys play basketball in here?" I asked.

"Yeah, but we also give customers a chance to save an extra 5 percent. You've got three tries; make a basket from that line over there and we'll cut 5 percent off the price. If you'd rather try your luck at golf, we've got a putter and ball and a cup."

I walked over and scooped up the B-ball. Positioning myself at the free-throw line, I bounced the ball twice, looked up with the intensity of a player facing a game-winning shot and arched the ball toward the rim. Swish! The round missile grazed the bottom of the net — too bad it didn't go in.

Again I settled in for a shot. The warehouse fell quiet. Customers, staff, family — all watched breathlessly as I rose to my toes for another exquisite release. As soon as the ball left my fingertips I knew, I just knew, it was going in. Swish. Five points!

We not only bought the carpet for Julie's room, the next day we came back and got a rug for Anna's room.

I never had so much fun buying carpet. In fact, I've been walking around our house looking at our worn carpet and thinking, *Hmmmmm, maybe I oughta go back and try for another 5-pointer!*

As we seek to *serve* our planned giving prospects, why not put a little fun into our work? Just think of the possibilities:

"Dunk the president in the tank and get an extra ticket to the recognition dinner."

"Pick the lowest card from the deck and have your gift annuity certificate framed in pewter."

"Throw the ball through the hoop and win a chance to give a three-minute testimonial at the next will's clinic."

Hey, let's lighten up and have a little fun.

18

Checklists

I love checklists. Don't know what I'd do without them. When I die, my tombstone will be etched with the words, "He was a Checklist Man."

Checklists remove ambiguity. They let me know exactly what needs to be done and where I am in the process. They liberate me from uncertainty. They lead me down the path of progress. They allow me to concentrate on other things.

Take, for example, the steps involved in receiving a charitable trust or gift annuity. Instead of trying to keep all of the many items ordered in my already overdrawn memory bank, I list them on a sheet and leave a line at the left of each item to mark down the date of completion.

I staple the checklist on the inside of the donor's folder where it's readily accessible. Then I place the folder in a holder near my desk. I don't have to wonder and worry where things are. I just reach over, pick out the donor's folder and look at the checklist.

Checklists can be developed for any recurring set of tasks. It may take time to sit down, think it all out and set up the list, but after that, it's peaches and cream. Checklists: You'll love them.

19
Dick's Office

I had not been to his office since he moved six years ago. He had willingly come to my home for insurance matters and I was always happy to give him that opportunity. But this time I went to see him.

I climbed the outside stairway to the second floor of a two-story building next to a busy thoroughfare. Finding his office, I opened the door. Inside I found a spacious room, with a high ceiling and shake walls on two sides. Live plants everywhere, like a garden.

Certificates and awards covered one wall. Impressive, but not overwhelming. Two work stations were strategically placed, one of them facing the door I entered. A couch and two easy chairs surrounded a large glass coffee table in the center of the room. And in the center of the table, a large spray of colorful flowers.

Before I could process all this, one of the secretaries came to me, extended her hand, and welcomed me to the office. She directed my gaze to an electronic readerboard on the desk in front of me. "Welcome Roger Schoenhals. We're glad you're here."

Saying that Dick was looking forward to seeing me and that he would be just a few minutes (I was early), she ushered me to the couch and pointed out the reading material. As I sat, she handed me a drink menu. The card listed coffee (regular and decaf), tea, a variety of soft drinks and various fruit juices.

The hostess secretary disappeared to bring the drink and the other secretary engaged me in light conversation. We joked about the readerboard and she told me how it worked. I said, "This is quite a place."

A young man in a side office came out and chatted briefly. He communicated friendliness and hospitality.

For the next five minutes or so, I sipped my drink, listened to music, looked around and relaxed. And I did some thinking. I thought of the hundreds of offices and waiting rooms I had encountered during my life. Nothing ever like this. Most of the time I feel like a number, an intrusion. Waiting rooms are often off to one side and either overly pretentious or awkwardly informal.

But here I was sitting comfortably in the middle of the operation, the focus of attention. Even though Dick knew my meeting with him was not to purchase a policy, the entire staff seemed genuinely glad to see me.

Dick interrupted my thoughts with a warm greeting and led me into a room other than his office — a comfortable place for talking and doing business. No cluttered desk, no walls dripping with diplomas, no telephone interruptions.

After our business I related my impressions of his outer office and of the attention I received. "We work hard on that," he said. "We try our best to let our clients know they're important to us . . . The staff understands that nothing they're doing at the time is more important than the guest who is in the room."

When I left the office that day, I turned back to see the readerboard on the desk. It said, "Have a good day."

Some of these things may seem a bit corny, but the fact is, they affected me in a positive manner. It's no wonder Dick is such a success.

I find myself thinking of ways to apply Dick's philosophy to my work in planned giving. What value do I place on the donors and prospects on my list? How far out of my way do I go to underscore, circle and highlight their value to me and to the organization I serve? Do I pamper only the heavy hitters, or do I treat everyone with sincere warmth and respect? What impression do they receive when they come to my office? What creative things can I do to say, "You are important to me"?

20
Helping With Our Ears

The couple greeted me at his office. In their early sixties, they had come to grips with their lack of planning and had invited me to help them "get our house in order." I readily disclosed my lack of professional standing in law, accounting and financial planning, and that my forte fell more in the area of charitable gift planning — but that I could provide some basic information and at least help them get started with their estate plan.

We talked for an hour and a half. Actually, for me it was more of an exercise in listening. As they got into the subject, they chattered and gestured excitedly. One would often jump in with an inspired thought before the other had completed a sentence. Periodically, they would turn to me and ask, "What do you think?" Before I could say 10 words they were off again chasing another thought.

It struck me, as I sat there, that this couple simply needed someone to serve as a catalyst, a focal point to get them going on a subject they had avoided all of their married lives. They rambled on about the pros and cons of leaving wealth to their sons, whether they needed more insurance, the merits of selling their house and moving into a condo. Even the possibility of leaving part of their estate to charity.

By the time I left, they were thanking me profusely for helping them. Helping them? Mostly, I just sat there and listened! Sometimes our ears are more effective than our tongues.

21
Recognition Mission

Seattle's Union Gospel Mission held a recognition event for those who had included the organization in their estate plans. We met at the main facility for lunch and a brief program. The director of development warmly welcomed the group, outlined the schedule of events and introduced the executive director who provided a brief update on recent developments. Then it was my turn to stroke the folks for their prudent investment in the future of the mission.

The centerpiece of the program featured a tour of the new youth center and a trip down to skid row to visit the remodeled men's shelter. As we shuffled from place to place, I noticed something taking place I had not fully anticipated: The members of the group seemed more interested in each other than the sights of the tour. They jabbered like long lost friends — though many had met for the first time. Repeatedly, we had to encourage them to "move along."

After we returned to the administrative facility, the group congregated outside the main door as though they wanted to prolong the experience before heading home. Quite unexpectedly, a rather shy elderly single man spoke up. "Say folks, gather around here. I want to tell you something."

He then related the following experience. A week or so earlier he had come out of a grocery store and met a man with a shopping cart of groceries. The stranger said he'd give him a couple of dollars if he would drive him the few blocks to his house. Innocently, our elderly friend helped the man put his groceries in the trunk and then drove him to the prescribed destination. Getting out to help unload the trunk, our friend suddenly witnessed the man jump behind the wheel of the car and speed off down the road.

A few days later the car was recovered, though badly damaged. Estimates ranged as high as $5,000 to repair the vehicle.

Our friend leaned into the group and exhorted them with a fervor I didn't know he possessed. "We have to beware of situations like this. We are good-natured and we want to help people in need. But we must be careful!"

It was really quite remarkable: Here was this man who, prior to the tour, had not known any of the other guests, expressing sincere concern for his new friends. He felt compelled to warn them of danger.

Later that evening I reflected on the day's activities. I felt good about several things. First, we provided an opportunity for the attendees to mix and converse. Instead of bringing them in and sitting them down for a program, and then sending them home, we created an opportunity for them to get acquainted.

Second, we focused on thanks. We made a point of affirming them without asking for more gifts. Yet, during the tour, at least three persons edged up to me and spoke about giving something more to the mission. Another person confided in me the amount of her designated bequest.

Third, we showed them results. During the tour, they not only saw the facilities, they saw and heard from individuals who had benefited from the mission's program. They met men who told their own stories about drug rehabilitation, job training, food and shelter assistance, and personal renewal. These firsthand encounters will linger longer than a dozen 20-minute "state of the work" speeches by the staff.

Fourth, we asked for their input. Along the way, we invited their comments. Consequently, we learned new things about Seattle and the early years of the 62-year-old mission. We also learned what these folks consider important.

Fifth, we announced the next event. We sent them home looking forward to the next time we would gather for food, conversation and a firsthand look at the mission.

Recognition events are opportunities to get people together who have a common commitment to our organizations. They are occasions to express sincere appreciation. They are chances to bring donors deeper into the soul of our cause. They are a means to cement revocable gifts and a way to inspire additional gifts. And they are times for fellowship and friend-making.

These recognition events are worth the effort.

22
Love Those Questions

Like most planned giving practitioners, I entered the field knowing next to nothing of what I was getting into. I was so green, a golf course looked pale by comparison. I didn't even know what questions to ask.

After attending the Kennedy Sinclaire program, a Sharpe institute and several Teitell seminars, I began putting some of the pieces together. Still, I felt bewildered most of the time. It helped to work through several gift arrangements. I also learned by reading the periodicals I received.

But what really made the difference for me was the day I decided to present a series of planned giving seminars to professional advisors. Not only did I have to get my thoughts outlined and polished, I had to anticipate any number of questions these experts might ask.

During the first few seminars, I found myself repeatedly saying, "That's a good question. Let me look into that and bring back the answer next time." Afterwards, I'd go to my office and search through what printed material I had accumulated. I'd get on the phone and harass my colleagues with my ignorance.

Over time, I learned to salute the difficult questions because they taught me what I needed to know. They led me deeper, honed my thinking. Instead of fearing the questions I learned to embrace them.

So I urge those of you who are just getting your feet wet to relish the questions. Welcome them. Invite them. Put yourself in situations where questions will arise, where you are forced to learn. Let the questions be your pathway to learning.

New letter rulings, different gift combinations, technical variations, marketing innovations — there's plenty to keep all of us scrambling. This is part of our grand adventure.

23
Furnaces and PS

Walking from our house to the mailbox at the curb, I noticed a furnace van in the driveway across the street. A phrase on the side panel caught my eye, "Planned Service." The phrase was next to a large, circled PS. And this logo was near to the name of the heating company.

I stood there for a moment, looking at the truck and pondering the PS message. Planned Service . . . Planned Giving. Hmmmmm. Our donors make planned gifts — we deliver planned service.

My neighbor later told me about their new gas furnace and the company that did the installation — the PS people. He said the planned service theme involved a series of regular contacts over a few years to make sure the furnace is working properly and the owners are satisfied.

Not a bad idea for us in planned giving. How about putting a service plan in place to ensure our donors that we are tracking them and continuing to care about their needs? Do we dare hand them a schedule of what they can expect over the next few years?

24
Which Attorney?

Last week I went to visit a childless, elderly couple who had called one of the charities I work with in the Seattle area. They had questions about revising their will and wanted my help.

I had never met them and they were basically unknown to the charity. Greeting me warmly, they ushered me to the dining room table. I sat down and the man placed a steaming hot cup of coffee and a homemade pastry before me (how I love this job!). Then the wife showed me copies of their outdated wills. She had clipped several handwritten notes to the sheets, indicating desired changes.

As I read through the material I discovered that they were making a change in the disposition of their estate because of a death in the family. I further noted that they were now naming "my" charity to receive most of their rather sizable estate. A marvelous revelation. Sometimes it's like that; it just seems to fall in your lap.

Their questions were fairly minor and I was able to cover them quickly. Then they informed me the attorney who had drawn their earlier will was no longer available and they needed a new one. Who would I suggest?

I was tempted to hook them up with one of my favorite attorneys, even deliver them to the office door. Instead, I followed my standard procedure.

First, I pointed out the importance of a *good* attorney, someone who was experienced in estate planning and probate matters. I drew the analogy between a foot doctor and a nose doctor. If you need a nose job, you don't go to a foot doctor.

Second, I urged them to talk with a trusted friend, perhaps someone who recently served as executor or even the person they plan to name as their executor. Ask for their advice. Find out who others are going to for these things.

Third, I gave them a list of three names, attorneys who I knew personally and could vouch for. The attorneys lived reasonably close, charged reasonable fees and had the expertise to handle this particular case. (Building a good network of estate planning attorneys pays off at times like this.)

Fourth, I helped them identify the questions they should ask the attorney and the information they should take to his or her office. I told them I wanted to make it as easy as possible for them and that I was available to assist them any way I could, even provide transportation if they desired.

They were very gracious and said they could take it from there. They also said they would send me a copy of the wills so the charity would have the information.

Good coffee, delicious pastry, a sizable estate, a copy of the wills . . . Is this living? Do chickens cluck?

25
When No Means Yes

Mr. Smith lives alone. He's a widower in his early 80s. When I call him to arrange for a visit, he characteristically says, "Please don't trouble yourself. I'm doing just fine. I'm sure you've got other things to do." But I go anyway because I've learned that, for Mr. Smith, no means yes.

Mrs. Jones is a widow in her 80s and also lives alone. She also says, "No, please don't come. But thank you for calling." Sometimes, I go anyway. And when I do, I sense her irritation in my coming against her wishes. When she said no, she meant it.

This business of being a planned giving officer requires a heap of discernment!

26
All Aboard!

The National Association of Church Business Administration met in Seattle for their 35th national conference. More than 550 members gathered to see the sights, listen to speakers, mingle with like-minded colleagues and attend workshops.

One of these workshops bore the title, "Planned Giving."

I wondered, *Will anyone attend my hour-and-a-half seminar? After all, there are so many great titles to choose from. Why would anyone walk down this long hall, past all of these other options, and turn into the only workshop room dealing with this subject? These are church administrators, why should they care about planned giving? I'll be lucky if three people show up.*

I tried out the overhead machine and laid some handouts on a few chairs. Then the person who was to introduce me arrived. I helped him pick out a few of the more salient points from the written information he had about me.

People began to arrive. More people. Would you believe 50? And the same thing happened in the afternoon when I repeated the workshop. Amazing! It just goes to show how pervasive our field is becoming.

Included in the introductory workshop was an illustration I have used a number of times to help people put planned giving in the proper context. Maybe it will come in handy for you sometime in a similar situation. Help yourself.

I start with an overhead transparency showing a crudely drawn train (something my younger daughter drew). It includes an engine, one train car and a caboose. Over the top is the heading, "The Planned Giving Train."

First, the engine. This is the power plant, the force that moves the train forward. I label the engine, "Charitable Desire." Then I go into a discourse about the importance of a gift being pulled along by a love for the charity, a commitment to its mission and a desire to help.

There are people in our constituencies who have identified themselves over time as loyal supporters. They've hung in there year after year. The idea is to stoke the furnace in their motivational engine and get that charitable intent burning hot. Focus on mission and need and the difference they have made — and can make.

This is the power that pulls the train.

Then I talk about the passenger cars, or the "Cars of Opportunity." There are several: remainder trusts, gift annuities, bequests, pooled income, insurance and so forth. I don't elaborate on any of these cars, but simply point them out as being there to serve as vehicles for charitable gifts.

Finally we come to the "Caboose of Benefit." This tag-along car carries the benefits we enjoy when we board one of the cars of opportunity, benefits like the satisfaction of making a major gift, the bypass of capital gains and a nice income tax deduction. But these, I explain, do not pull the train.

Trying to move a train down the tracks by the caboose is like putting the cart before the horse. Let the caboose lead and we all go backward.

I talk about selfish giving vs. altruistic giving and the values of building on the latter. Nothing is sweeter than helping a donor who really wants to help give more than he or she imagined possible. A few cautions about marketing planned gifts as tax "shelters" may be appropriate here.

Then I haul out an example of a highly motivated couple who got on the charitable remainder unitrust car and the good ride they enjoyed. A series of overheads presents the step-by-step process of making such a planned gift and the benefits that follow. If time permits, other "cars of opportunity" could be explored.

Sometimes I include other things in my "Planned Giving Train" talk. Like the planned giving landscape the train passes through (giving conditions of the '90s). Or the stations where the train stops to pick up eager travelers with appreciated property, or those with retirement needs.

The analogy can be carried out ad infinitum. You can even get so wrapped up in the presentation that you conclude with a hearty, "All Aboard!"

My morning workshop went overtime. In fact, a man stuck his head in the door and said, "The people are sitting down for lunch." I was the first one out the door.

After the afternoon seminar, several people lingered and we talked for another 30-45 minutes about planned giving in the local church and how they could get a little planned giving committee started and some of the resources available to them.

Did I tell them about *Planned Giving Today* and how this practical newsletter might help them? Do cows mooooo?

27
Leftovers

You work hard to promote bequests. You give seminars, write articles, send brochures and place notices in your publications. And then, out of the blue, an envelope arrives from an attorney announcing "The Notice of Appointment and Pendency of Probate." A copy of the will is enclosed. The name is unfamiliar.

Your hands tremble as your mind formulates the image of a huge bequest. Your body quivers. You sit down. You turn to the first page of the will to find the name of your organization. Nothing, except an outright bequest to an individual for $5,000.

You turn the page. You find eight paragraphs, each awarding an individual either $5,000 or $1,000. At the bottom of the page you read, "All the rest, residue and remainder of my estate, I hereby give, devise and bequeath as follows:

"1. One-tenth (1/10) of my estate I hereby give to the _____ Church for general purposes."

Your heartbeat quickens. You think, *Maybe the rest is ours? If not, even if we only get one-tenth that will be okay. A million dollars? Maybe more* . . . . Your imagination jumps the fence and races to the open fields of a multi-million dollar bequest.

You turn to page three. There you find nine paragraphs numbered 2-10, each awarding 10 percent of the residue to an individual. Hey! Where's your organization?

You return to page one and two and then back to three. You count the 10 paragraphs that, together, give away the entire residue of the estate.

You sense a tidal wave of disappointment moving toward your sand castle of expectation.

Scanning down the remaining paragraphs of the will, you find these words: "In the event my personal representative shall be unable (within a nine (9) month period from my death) to sell or liquidate all of my household or personal items, I hereby direct that she give them to _____, and receive a receipt therefrom."

The wave crashes, rolls up the beach and . . .

28
Automated Gratitude

The checkout clerk rings up my groceries, takes my money, hands me the change, and says, "Thank you for shopping at _____."

Only she doesn't mean it. I can tell because of the weary, automated tone of her voice — and because she's looking toward the next customer as she speaks.

Saying "thank you" to customers is probably company policy. And I suppose at first she said it thoughtfully and with a smile. But as the days and weeks passed, the practice became a habit, and the habit became a mechanical response.

Our company policy, as planned giving officers, is to repeatedly express gratitude to our donors for their generous gifts, gifts that may have been made years before. But, like the woman at the checkout counter, we can become careless and cold, mouthing words as we contemplate our next visit. Just going through the motions.

So how do we remain fresh and genuine in the giving of thanks? By looking people in the eye and by elaborating on the reasons for our gratitude.

29
Good Timing

I was helping a local charity establish a planned giving program. To get us going with a few marketing brochures, I filled out an order form and sought approval. I wanted something to give as a follow-up to direct mail activities and to distribute at an upcoming seminar. The brochures covered wills, life-income agreements and basic estate planning.

I went over my selections with the director of development. He winced noticeably when he saw the cost of the imprinted brochures. He suggested we pare down the total number for this first order. "That's fine," I said. "Whatever we can get will be helpful."

The next day my phone rang and the director of development excitedly told me of a large check they had just received from an estate. Everyone at the charity was singing songs of joy.

And then he said, "Why don't you go ahead and order the full number of brochures you need. We want to get this planned giving program up and running."

Good timing makes a big difference!

A wise planned giving officer will have proposals in a desk drawer to pull out when word comes of a windfall estate gift. He or she will also make sure that everyone inside the organization knows when a gift matures. News of a completed gift is a dandy way to communicate the value of your planned giving program.

To make sure you cover the bases, try this: Establish a checklist of every news outlet relevant to the staff and constituency of your organization. When a deferred gift matures, write a news release and instruct your secretary to get it out according to the checklist.

Another idea: Plan a signing ceremony for every trust, annuity, pooled income fund addition and new endowment. Do it in the president's office and arrange for a photographer. This will not only affirm the donor and give you a photo and quotes for a news release, it will confirm the importance of your program to the executives you serve. Keeping them happy and positive about your program will benefit you when budget time rolls around.

A completed gift agreement or a matured gift creates a window of opportunity. We can use these times to further our cause, or we can let the moment pass. Good timing means grasping the opportunity.

30
And the Gift Goes On

I'm holding here a letter my parents recently received from the planned giving director of a college they support in upstate New York. Several months ago they gave a charitable gift annuity to the college and the story had been reported in the school's planned giving newsletter. The letter relates the influence of that article in bringing about a gift annuity from another person. It says, "Without question your story played a major role in inspiring this major endowment gift . . . . Thank you for allowing your story to be told that others might do likewise."

It wasn't necessary for the PGO to dictate the letter. Most of us would probably overlook the opportunity. But his act of kindness affirmed my parents and set the stage for another gift.

I'm thinking, *This guy is on the ball.*

31
The Low Road

Today I visited a widower in his late 80s. No kids. An estate worth one million dollars. He wants to create a living trust and use his accountant, a CPA, as successor trustee. He's also considering a $400,000 unitrust, though he has yet to discuss this with his CPA. He intends to give his CPA durable power of attorney. The CPA will be responsible for the health and welfare of the elderly man should he require custodial care. The CPA lives down the block and works out of his house.

Once, not long ago, the Salvation Army brought the elderly gentleman a charitable gift proposal. Not a big one, but enough to generate a tax deduction worth $5,000. He took the proposal to his accountant for advice. "Why do you want to do this," asked the professional advisor. "What's the Salvation Army ever done for you?"

And then the CPA presented this alternative: "Why don't you just let me bill you $5,000 for doing your tax return and then you can deduct *this* from your taxes?" Ughhh!

32
The High Road

A friend of mine, an attorney, told me of the time an elderly widow offered him a large sum of money. She had come to his office for some estate planning and wanted his advice on what to do with her money, both now and in the future. She had no children. Finally, she said, "Here, let me write you a check for $100,000. You will use it better than anyone else I know. Your kids could use some help with college. Why don't you just let me give this money to you?"

Had he been of a different stripe, he might have taken the money and used it on himself. No one would have been the wiser. After all, who couldn't use an extra hundred grand?

Instead, he probed her background and uncovered an interest which he coaxed into the foreground. He presented some giving options and helped her weigh the pros and cons. Then, on her own, she chose to use the money to establish an endowment fund where it could benefit young people for generations to come. Her satisfaction in making this gift brought him immense delight. You would think he made the gift himself!

The reason the attorney told me this story was to illustrate the temptations he and other estate planning professionals face when dealing with generous and vulnerable clients. He reminded me that personal and professional ethics are not concerns only of planned giving officers but of everyone who takes seriously the weighty role of assisting others with their estates.

This attorney, and others like him, give their profession a good name. Add to them the CPAs, stockbrokers, insurance professionals and financial planners who carry out their work with the highest standards of professionalism and ethics, and you have a network of men and women who are not only worth knowing, but worth working with in the gift-planning arena.

To all of you estate planning professionals who walk the high road, I tip my hat. We in the planned giving profession appreciate you.

33

Bitten by the Bug

I took the director of development with me to make a few calls. I wanted him to meet some donors who had recently included our organization in their wills.

The highlight of the afternoon came as we sat in a lovely home with a couple in their 80s. They had stipulated in their wills that the house and some other valuable assets would come to our organization at their death. The husband told us about the recent improvements to the house and called our attention to the lovely landscaping in the backyard — a product of his wife's handiwork, he said.

As they reflected on their years in the house, my companion suddenly came forward in his chair as though he had seen a vision. "You know," he began, "It just occurred to me that what you are giving away is much more than a house. This is your home! These walls contain memories of happy times and sad times. This is where you sleep and eat and entertain and where you share long intimate conversations. You are giving us something much more than wood and nails; this house is part of you. Giving stock or cash is one thing, but to give your home is truly a precious gift. We are deeply grateful."

The director's insight captured the moment. He had grasped something of the profound meaning of their decision. And in so doing, he had discovered something awesome about planned giving — the means by which our donors pass to us their most treasured assets.

The husband wanted to know what would become of the house. Would we rent it out as income property? Would we use it for staff housing? I explained it was likely we would work with a reputable realtor in finding a fine family to purchase the house. We would then take the proceeds and invest them in the organization in a way that would help us fulfill our mission. Both spouses seemed pleased with this prospect. They liked the idea that their home would continue to be a home and that the organization they had supported for so many years would be strengthened for even greater service.

I will not soon forget the look on the director's face when the insight dawned and he began to expound about their "ultimate" gift. I think I saw a person bitten by the planned giving bug.

34
Partial to Print

Whatever else you have going in your planned giving program, you'll do better if you make print a part of your plans. Use a newsletter or booklet to tell the story of donors who have made planned gifts. List the how-to steps. Put the power of print to work for you.

Print respects human freedom. Instead of forcing one to follow the mechanical pace of an audio or video tape, print lets the reader lead. Go as fast or as slow as you want. Stop mid-sentence to think. Print encourages thought and resolve.

Print is portable. A newsletter or booklet may be placed in a pocket or purse for ready use at those unexpected idle times. It can be passed easily to a friend or family member — or sent across the country through the mail.

Print promotes understanding. Putting words on paper forces you to think through the subject. The more you write about it, the better you know it. The same is true of your readers. Keep your prospects supplied with printed material, well-written and attractively presented, and understanding will begin to seep through.

Print develops credibility. There's something about the printed word that carries a hint of authority. People tend to believe what they read.

Print multiplies your efforts. You can extend yourself through the written word. You can have as many "representatives" out there as your publication budget allows.

Print goes on and on. Once unleashed in print, your comments will outlive you. They will turn up in unexpected places at unexpected times. They will work for you tirelessly.

I'm partial to print. It works.

35
Artful Juxtaposition

I have here a copy of a newspaper page from a subscriber in Virginia containing two prominent display ads side-by-side. On the left is a picture of Billy Graham and notice of his sermon topic for an upcoming telecast: "Is the End of the World Close?" To the right of this is an equally commanding ad by the Rockingham (Virginia) Memorial Hospital and Foundation, announcing: "Your Estate: How to Plan It." Nice placement, huh?

36
A Few Resolutions

I'm a sucker for New Year's resolutions. Seems like I always come up with a list longer than my arm. In case you're running short, here are a few of my perennial favorites.

I Will Give My Undivided Attention. When you're in conversation with another person, focus on them completely, exclusively, wholeheartedly. Don't let your eyes or mind wander. Let the person know by your attentiveness that you value them and truly want to know what they think. I had a prof in college who was a master at this. Would that I could develop this skill to such a degree.

I Will Foster an Attitude of Gratitude. My mother was good at this. She was thankful for everything, for everybody, for every day . . . and she knew how to express it. She delighted in sending cheerful notes and making uplifting phone calls — all spiced with gratitude. When she thanked you for doing something, you knew you had been thanked. What a tremendous quality for gift planners.

I Will Do My Work Enthusiastically. Make a list of things you can affirm in your work and then begin to express enthusiasm about these things, even forcing yourself if necessary. In the process of verbalizing your enthusiasm, positive forces are unleashed and you will begin to feel better about your work, better about yourself and better about those around you. What's more, others will feel better about you. As N.V. Peale says, "Enthusiasm makes the difference."

So . . . enthusiastically speaking, let me give you my undivided attention and tell you that I am sincerely thankful you are taking the time to read this!

37
Three More Resolutions

Another year has come and gone and it's resolution time again. Here are three more I intend to work on this new year:

I Will Hobnob With Positive People. Like most of you, I'm affected by the attitudes of others. Down-in-the-mouth people depress me. If I hang around them too long, my perspective droops. But enthusiastic, go-get-em types charge my batteries. They help me maintain a positive mental attitude . . . and PMA breeds success.

I Will Dispense Encouragement. Like I told my daughter when I dropped her off at middle school this morning, "Leave every person you talk with today a better person." And what better way to lift others than to encourage them along the way? The new year will be satisfying if we daily issue words of encouragement through conversation, notes, cards, letters, phone calls and, yes, faxes and e-mail. Let the good words flow!

I Will Hug My Organization. It's hard to enjoy planned giving when you lack zeal for your cause. After all, how can you convince others if your own conviction wanes? To keep your passion strong, open your arms and embrace anew the distinctives of your organization. Revisit the mission; ponder the dreams of the founders. The closer you hold your institution, the more you will love your job.

Have a great year!

38
A Pause That Refreshes

I am floating down the Colorado River on a private float trip through the Grand Canyon. I have been living a stressful life as the editorial director of a publishing house in the Midwest and I need this time to relax.

The second night out I unroll my sleeping bag on a flat, sandy spot a few feet from the river. I stretch out and immediately fall into anxious thoughts about my hectic life. With furrowed brow, I review deadlines, meetings and unfinished projects. I grow more tense by the moment.

And then, mercifully, something happens to change my perspective. My mind perceives what my eyes see. I behold a star-splattered sky framed by the ancient canyon walls. The splendor of the universe seeps into my fretful mind.

And then I realize that 10 feet away rolls the mighty Colorado, silently and ceaselessly cutting deeper, deeper into the earth. A sense of awe sweeps over me. I am in the workshop of the Creator. He is carving Himself a canyon.

And He isn't in a hurry.

Sometimes it's good to step back and take a deep breath. We can become so caught up in the pressures and responsibilities of our work that we rush anxiously here and there as though the world will collapse if we pause. The Milky Way above and the Grand Canyon below teach us differently.

39
Looking Good

Jim is an attorney in Seattle and a member of the Washington Planned Giving Council. He was one of three speakers at a recent council meeting who presented a program titled, "Working With PGOs: Three Professional Advisors Speak Out."

Jim told of a client who wanted to make a deferred gift to an organization and how the planned giving officer, who was in the audience, had been so helpful in providing information and general support. At the close of his talk, Jim looked over to the PGO and said, "Thanks, Dick, for making me look so good."

There was genuine appreciation in the attorney's voice and you could tell he would not hesitate to involve the planned giving officer in another gift plan. One could even imagine that he might steer a charitably minded client toward Dick just to have the pleasure of looking good.

A PGO is no fool who elevates the client's advisor during the gift-planning process.

40
Birthday Party Madness

Robert Frost wrote, "Spring is the mischief in me." Well, me too. This is the time of year I get a wee bit silly. Take, for example, the office birthday party I attended a few years ago. Among the gifts was my creation: a large, heavy wooden crate. It was fastened together with giant screws.

Having fetched a screwdriver and hammer, the middle-aged honoree opened the box . . . only to find a second container inside, similarly sealed. Inside this box, he found styrofoam peanuts surrounding a smaller container. Like opening a series of

Russian dolls, the poor soul kept "digging" deeper and deeper, looking for his gift. Finally, he came upon a short pipe welded shut at both ends. After cutting through the pipe with a hacksaw, my (former) friend discovered 45 pennies — one for each year of his life.

Yep, "Spring is the mischief in me."

41

The Annuity Connection

Meet Andy Nuitant. That's not his real name, of course. But it might as well be. He has more annuities than anyone else I know.

I first met Andy when I began my planned giving work for a university here in Seattle. During the early weeks, I made the rounds to get acquainted with the trustors, annuitants and others who had made a deferred gift. Andy was on my list.

Andy, I discovered, had been a widower for several years. He lives in a retirement complex in Tacoma, a city several miles to the south. During our first visit I learned that he not only had a gift annuity with my university, but with two other local universities and at least two charitable organizations.

What's more, Andy has more than one annuity with most of the institutions and organizations. And he is adding more. None of the annuities are large, but together they add up to a sizable amount.

Andy is not an alumnus of the universities, nor affiliated in a special way with the charities. Why, then, all the annuities?

Over time, I learned the answer. First, Andy is alone. He is nearly 90 and most of his friends are gone. He uses a gift annuity to tie himself to nearby organizations he feels good about. This tie creates an interest bank, providing him with a flow of incoming materials through the mail and with a wide assortment of events to attend. The organizations have become "his" and he delights in keeping up with all the developments.

His annuity connection also provides a stream of visitors. I made a point of visiting him occasionally, not only to affirm his generosity, but to encourage further gifts.

Andy would tell me about the other organizations and who had been to see him. Whether intended or not, his reference to my "competition" made me determined to keep my link with him strong. I knew that others would be calling on him and I wanted to make sure he was kept up-to-date on our institution. (Andy is no fool.)

As I got acquainted with my counterparts at the two other universities, we shared our thoughts about our most enthusiastic annuitant. The three of us learned to enjoy our common ties with Andy.

When my institution held our annual Heritage Club reception, Andy would be there front and center. Once, when we were unable to provide transportation, Andy boarded a bus and made the trip alone. We made sure he received a personal ride home.

Andy's wife and friends are gone, but the institutions he has gathered around himself will not disappear. He can count on these connections right through to the end. They add stability to his life.

If we offer prospective donors an ongoing connection with us and the organizations we represent, if we facilitate relationships with other like-minded donors, if we provide a flow of interesting information and activity opportunities, if we supply sincere appreciation and warm-hearted affirmation, and if we serve as a stabilizing force in the sunset years, we make it easy for annuity and trust gifts to come our way.

Planned giving is more than getting something for our organizations. It's giving back to the donor a supportive, lifelong connection. Insurance companies offer annuities; investments offer interest; but we offer so much more.

42
The Second Mile

I knew I was in trouble when the elderly widow on the phone gave me garbled instructions on how to get to her apartment. "Just give me the address," I pleaded. "I'm sure I can find it." "You don't need the address if you follow my instructions." And then she went through them again, providing conflicting information with her earlier directions.

Mrs. Jones had been part of the organization since it began 25 years ago and had recently learned of my involvement as the new planned giving officer. She wanted to meet me.

Fifteen miles down the road, I realized I had left her address on my desk. Knowing I was heading in the right direction, I called her on my car phone for the address. Seemed simple enough.

Trying to scribble down her instructions while zooming along the freeway taxed my coordination. "Call me when you get in the parking lot and I'll come down and show you the way to my apartment," she directed.

"OK, but I wish you would give me the address so I'll be sure to drive into the right parking lot."

"If you follow my instructions, you'll drive right here."

Putting the pieces together as best I could, I found what I thought was the right lot. Then I called and told her I was there. Then I waited. And waited. I got out and walked around. I scanned the mailbox names at the entrance of the apartment building for her name. I asked people who came out the door whether they knew her. No luck.

I was walking back to my car to call her again, when I noticed a rather perturbed lady striding toward me from an adjoining parking lot. Whoops.

Falling over myself with apologies, I was able to ease her annoyance at my inability to follow instructions. Still apologizing, I helped her into my car and we drove over to the correct lot.

Seated at her small dining table, I learned more about the purpose of my visit. "Well I'm glad they're finally doing something about us older folk," she said. "We've needed somebody like you to help us." And with that, she began placing in front of me a mound of bank statements, bills, overdraft notices, quarterly reports and other business papers — some of it dating back three years, some of it unopened.

"I want you to help me get all of this stuff organized."

For a good hour I sorted through the mess, creating little piles here and there, all the while listening to her life story. I thought, *How do I tell this lady that I can't be her personal business manager?*

"I've got a burial plot down at the cemetery I'd like to see. Haven't been there for 30 years. Will you drive me? It'll only take a few minutes."

"Well, er, ah, er . . . "

We got in the car and headed toward town. "Are you sure you know where we're going? Do you know the address?"

She assured me vehemently.

After three stops to ask directions, two attempted phone calls and a rather intense session with a local map, I found the cemetery. She waited in the car while I went in the office to get the location of her plot. They had her name on the books, but her plot was under the new office building and she would need to select a new one. The director said, "We sent her a letter some time ago about this."

Mercifully, Mrs. Jones decided to wait for another day before selecting a new plot. She wanted to think about it and to maybe come back with one of her friends.

Back in the apartment house parking lot, I was led to her car. "It's been sitting there for a long time. Needs to be started up now and then. Here's the key. Crank it up for me, will ya?"

I turned the key and . . . dead battery. My heart sank. I revived when she said she'd have someone from the corner service station take care of it.

"Before you go, will you come in for a piece of pie? Just a couple of minutes."

At this point, an involuntary mechanism in my stomach took control and I reentered her apartment. She pushed back the piles of papers and brought out a peach pie. We both had a generous slice. And then we both had another one.

We started to laugh together about the directions and the cemetery fiasco and the dead battery. I thought, *What a wonderful sense of humor this lady has!*

We talked about her business affairs and the need to have someone help her on a regular basis. She had a person in mind, a close friend who had helped her in the past.

By the time I left (agreeing to return sometime for another piece of pie), we were pals. I had learned about her fondness for the organization and that she had included us in her will. I also had been reminded that sometimes an older person will test you to find out whether you — and the organization you represent — really care.

43
Gift Planner's Dilemma

Our local planned giving council provided a program last week on the subject, "Working With Older Donors." Five members of the program committee presented case studies and helpful advice. As good as it was, however, the best part of the gathering for me was a conversation I had prior to lunch with one of the attendees, a trust officer with a local bank.

I asked Mike about an elderly gentleman we both knew, a man in his early 90s. "How's he doing? Is he getting out much?" I asked.

"Not much," he said. "All his friends are dead. His only contacts with the outside world are the charitable organizations he cares about. He really loves to have representatives come and visit him."

That brief conversation haunted me throughout the meal and the program. I reflected on the larger role of the planned giving officer — a role so often unappreciated by the employing organization. Surely, planned giving properly extends beyond the acquisition of gifts to the planned giving of our time and care to those elderly supporters who have made multiple gifts to our organization. Are we only to seek the next gift? Or are we also to spend time being friends to lonely seniors who are part of our donor "family"? How much time can we afford to give away? Does our organization have a moral obligation to walk alongside these people during their final years, these who are looking to our organization for stability and friendship? Where is the line between fund raising and care-giving?

44
Flinging the Seed

A man came to see me last week who was getting ready to sell several properties. He had heard bits and pieces about planned giving and wanted to find out about these charitable alternatives. We talked at length and I fully expect one or more gift plans will materialize.

What fascinated me about our conversation is the importance of those little bits of information he had absorbed over time. Newsletters, articles, brochures, presentations — they all had done their job. Though he didn't understand the details, he knew there was a way to benefit himself and his charity through proper planning.

While target marketing has its place in planned giving, it cannot replace the need for faithful, continual planting in the open fields of our constituencies. Like Johnny Appleseed, we can plant the good seed of planned giving wherever we go. Or like the farmer in the field, we can walk the furrows and fling out the seed all around.

As we broadcast the little kernels, some will fall on good ground. The rains will come and the seed will germinate. Roots will shoot down into the fertile soil. And, eventually, a gift will appear. And another. And another.

45
When PGOs Cry

Today I saw a grown man cry — almost. His voice quavered as he recounted the frustration of trying to get a major planned gift in the door. For the past several months he has been working with a motivated donor to create a $500,000 charitable remainder unitrust. The unencumbered real estate has been appraised and the environmental audit completed.

The title search is done and the trust and transfer papers have been drawn — all at the donor's expense. A buyer is standing in the wings. The whole thing is a slam dunk.

Like preparing for a wedding, graduation or some other climactic event, the donor has moved forward with mounting excitement over the creation of this gift. All is ready. Both he and the planned giving officer are emotionally keyed for completion.

Enter the gift acceptance committee. The chairman, a volunteer, is out of town for a week. He is booked solid when he returns and can't meet for another week. The other two members don't want to proceed on their own. And even though the trust is a net-income-only arrangement and the skids are greased for acceptance, the institution's finance department is suddenly skittish about "rushing" into such a big gift.

The planned giving officer is caught in the middle. He has brought the gift to the door, where he stands, seeking entrance.

He must keep the donor pumped up while trying to create a sense of urgency among his conservatively minded, slow-moving associates.

My friend is on the verge of tears because he can't do anymore than he's done and he fears that the unnecessary delay in accepting the gift will discourage the donor and undo all the efforts of the past few months.

A gift acceptance committee which doesn't understand the importance of timing and donor dynamics, or committee members who are so busy with their own affairs that they can't respond quickly when the crucial moment comes, is a liability to success. And a cause for tears.

46
Shortsighted Savings

Yesterday a colleague told me of a friend in another state who had been called into the vice president's office and told that the university's planned giving program was shutting down and that his position was to be eliminated . . . immediately.

I recalled a similar story involving a friend of mine who worked at a local hospital. A year ago, he too had been abruptly dismissed because the board decided to ax the program.

A third situation, quite recent, involves another friend who also was directing the planned giving program at a hospital. She was called into a meeting and informed that her position was being terminated. No more planned giving.

All three of these cases (and you can think of others) involved talented planned giving persons who were dedicated to their work and who were involved in leadership roles in the larger planned giving community. They had been on the job for several years, had built strong relationships on behalf of their organizations, and had been successful in acquiring planned gifts. All three were terminated because the budget, reportedly, could no longer carry the planned giving program.

I confess to a bit of rage. I'm angry at the way these dismissals were handled. I'm angry at the shortsightedness of those who bear responsibility for the future of these organizations. I'm angry at the loss of all those wasted years of building relationships and credibility.

Some prevention is in order. It may be prudent for planned giving officers to continually circulate planned giving articles among board members and top executives. Send them updates announcing the arrival of a bequest or the signing of a new planned gift.

Invite a board member to be your guest at a planned giving council meeting. Take various members with you on donor visits. Encourage board members to attend recognition events. Introduce a recent donor at a board meeting.

Never let your board and chief executive forget the great work you are doing on their behalf and how vital planned giving is for the future life and health of their organization. Be proactive!

47
Stair Peak

A year or so ago I noticed him at the community park two blocks from our house, a forty-ish man in a grey sweatsuit climbing stairs. His face, etched with determination, revealed a serious get-back-in-shape midlifer who was using the stairs as a conditioning tool. An Irish setter sat at the base looking up at the man who huffed and puffed his way up and down the three flights of stairs.

The next day I observed the man doing the same thing. Also the dog.

For most of the year, if I'd drive past those stairs at a certain morning hour, the man would be there doing his ups and downs. And always the dog.

The sight of this guy painting the stairs with his sweat began to haunt me. I wanted to stop and talk with him and discover the who and why. I also began to feel guilty when I saw him, shamed I wasn't out there hauling my own body up and down the hill.

Driving away from the stairs, I'd reflect on his discipline. Rain or shine, he was out there pushing himself to the limit. Such determination, such will power. What an inspiration!

Then, suddenly, the stair climber disappeared. And the dog. I watched for them during the next couple of weeks, only to find the stairs empty. I developed some concerns. Is he okay? Did he move? Why did he stop? Where's the dog?

I mulled over these perplexing questions for days. And then, as though led by some great mysterious force, I put on my tennis shoes and headed for the stairs. I climbed and counted. The first flight had 24 and the next two had 27 each. Seventy-eight concrete stairs.

I came down, turned around and headed up. Not bad, I thought. I did it again. And again.

Today, two months later, I'm doing 26 round trips several days a week. That's more than 2,000 stairs a shot. I'm even thinking of getting a dog.

What's more, I've worked out a little scheme. I "hike" up the stairs one at a time for 15 round-trips. This is like the foothills on my way to climb the mountain peak. Next, I take two stairs at a time for seven round trips. It's steeper because I'm getting farther up the mountain. For the next three trips I take three steps at a time. Now I'm nearly there, I can see the summit.

But the last 500 feet is a killer — a four-stair stretch. My pulse is banging away and my shirt is drenched in sweat. No turning back. With all the gusto I can muster, I go for the final ascent and force myself up the stairs one last time.

Gaining the summit, I stagger around gasping for air. But, oh, how sweet it is. The view is fantastic and I feel like I'm on top of the world. I conquered Stair Peak!

What does all of this have to do with planned giving? Stay with me. Let's see if I can squeeze something out.

First, consider the power of example. People are moved to action by the positive activity of others. Tell the stories often enough of donors who have made planned gifts and you'll have new donors coming out of the woodwork.

Second, the planned giving profession can be a lonely hike and you may need to develop a scheme to keep yourself motivated. Try a system of short and long range goals.

Third, imagine yourself on the summit of a newly acquired planned gift and then take the steps necessary to get there.

Fourth, get a dog.

48
Drip, Drip

My October 4 planned giving seminar was promoted in the usual manner: notices in two successive newsletters, distribution of flyers, letters to key prospects, personal invitation to the board of trustees, news releases to appropriate media, and various other public announcements.

Eighteen persons called to reserve space. But only nine prospects came. The seven staff members brought the total to 16.

We held the seminar in one of the facilities operated by the sponsoring charity. The spacious, carpeted room was well-prepared with tables and chairs, overhead, sound system and a refreshment table loaded with freshly baked pastries (cherry cake, chocolate cake, cheese cake, rolls, etc.). A literature table offered an array of newly acquired brochures and attractive literature about the organization. Neatly placed program outlines and other handouts defined the seating arrangements.

Nine guests! I told myself it only took one nice estate gift to make the seminar worthwhile. Then I thought, *The important thing here is that we're serving these donors and friends of the charity and whether we receive any gifts as a direct result of this seminar is not the issue.* That thought helped me. It also helped to look out the window and see buckets of rain coming down. I told myself this had something to do with the low attendance.

Our schedule called for refreshments and conversation from 1:30 p.m. to 1:40 p.m. This allowed time for any latecomers to arrive before we started the program. At 1:40 p.m., the director of development welcomed the group and made a few introductions. Then, from 1:45 p.m. to 1:55 p.m., I gave a brief introduction to the overall subject matter.

During the next 50 minutes, an estate planning attorney gave an excellent introduction to the basic tools of estate planning. Midway through his presentation, a drop of water descended and landed on his head. And then another drop. And another. Finally, he moved.

One of the staff members hurried out to find a pail. Once in place, the pail acted as a sound chamber for each exploding drop. Then the staff person located a towel to put in the pail to muffle the sound. All the while, the attorney continued his discourse on wills, durable powers of attorney and the relative merits of a revocable trust. When he concluded, we gathered at the refreshment table and joked together about the rain, the leak and the hapless victim.

Then it was my turn. With coffee cups and napkins of food adorning the table space of each listener, I began my 50-minute oration on planned giving. Mysteriously, the dripping stopped. (Hmmmmm.)

I took them through a few scenarios, using the overhead and handouts. Several questions interrupted my presentation. "Who serves as the trustee of these trusts?" "How much does it take to start a trust?" The people seemed interested.

At 3:40 p.m. the development director wrapped things up. He reminded them of the materials on the table and requested that the seminar evaluation form be completed, including the question regarding a follow-up visit.

For several minutes, the guests lingered to ask questions and to chat with one another. They indicated appreciation for the event and some even apologized for the low attendance. While no one expressed a commitment to make an estate gift because of the seminar, good will prevailed and new ideas found fertile soil. Perhaps the drip, drip of further cultivation will moisten the soil and cause the good seed to sprout. Time will tell.

49
Gratification and Character

After my presentation on the benefits of launching a planned giving program, I learned something from one of the attendees — something now incorporated in my lecture notes. During the discussion time, he spoke of a planned giving program having the power to infuse an organization with character.

The annual campaign, he said, stresses the day-in and day-out financial needs of the organization. Give money now and help meet our needs. Instant benefit results from the gift — for both donor and nonprofit. Immediate gratification.

A planned giving program, with its emphasis on deferred gifts and future needs, breaks the monotonous cycle of the annual campaign by cutting a bold line into the future. Give now; help later. Gratification deferred.

One form of giving provides instant resources; the other requires patience and discipline. And patience produces character. And character spawns stability and confidence.

Is it too strong to suggest that an organization without a planned giving program is consigned to a stunted existence? And, can we not say that the organization with an effective planned giving program is more likely to depict depth and direction?

According to this perspective, we who labor as gift planners are doing nothing less than building institutional character.

50
Such a Great Profession

Today, while driving home from our planned giving council meeting, I considered the benefits of the planned giving profession. Interstate 5 was crowded, but the traffic moved along nicely. I drove in the center lane.

I thought about the *purpose* of our profession. We are in the business of assisting others to give. We are guides, enablers. We unlock giving opportunities by solving problems of appreciation, inadequate income and family concerns. We bring happiness by showing people that they really can make a major gift.

We also enable the charitable causes people support. We're on the cutting edge, acquiring funds for the future. We assist in building the vast network of nonprofit enterprises throughout this great land.

Second, I considered the *people* of our profession. There are the donors. If they are properly motivated, helping them is fun. They get excited about the gift and they appreciate our help. Good givers make great friends.

And there are the like-minded associates, people not only in planned giving and related development fields, but those special people in the allied professions who have caught the planned giving bug. Our profession draws persons who are enjoyable to be around. To paraphrase Will Rogers, "I never met a gift-planning professional I didn't like."

A third reason I like planned giving is the *promise* of our profession. The future is bright. While other professions battle lethargy, we're in the springtime of life. Fresh talent is flowing into our ranks. Opportunities abound for training. Job openings and compensation are on the rise.

Fourth, I enjoy the *pulse* of our profession. There's a mood of excitement, a feeling of being part of something tremendous. Planned giving training seminars and national conferences are marked by enthusiasm and lively interchange.

Unlike some professions that struggle for a place in the sun, we're riding high the crest of new beginnings. The heartbeat of our profession is strong.

My thoughts about the good things of planned giving screeched to a halt when a car to the right of me moved toward my lane. I hit the breaks and applied the horn. The invading car continued into my space and went on down the road in front of me. The driver appeared oblivious to the collision he nearly caused.

Our profession, vital and promising, is humming down the road. We're traveling in the center of the professional interstate. While enjoying the purpose, people, promise and pulse of our profession, let's not lose sight of the *perils*.

To the right and the left are potential dangers. We must keep our eyes on the road. Make smooth transitions. Flow with traffic. Stay in our lane. Check the mirror. Be vigilant. Drive skillfully and defensively. And we must keep our vehicle in good condition.

The perils are part of our journey. But the ride and scenery make it all worthwhile. The planned giving profession is going places and I'm glad to be on board. How about you?

51
Deferred Recognition

Not everyone likes to hear a drum roll when they sign on the dotted line. Take Mr. X, for example. After he signed the unitrust documents, he excused himself and tried to slip away. But I went after him and told him again of our gratitude for his generous gift. I wanted him to feel appropriately appreciated.

Then I asked whether I could share the good news. I said, "Do you mind if we tell others about your gift? I'd like to write an article for our newsletter and explain what you did and why you did it. I believe it will encourage others to follow your example. Your gift may prompt others. What do you say . . . may I proceed?"

He would not have it. In fact, he asked that we not tell anyone about his gift. "I want it to be anonymous," he said. And then he added with utmost seriousness, "I don't want to lose my reward."

Reward? What reward? He studied the question marks in my eyes for a moment. And then, quoting from the Bible, he said, "Be careful not to do your 'acts of righteousness' before men, to be seen by them. If you do, you will have no reward from your Father in heaven . . . . When you give to the needy, do not let your left hand know what your right hand is doing, so that your Father, who sees what is done in secret, will reward you."

The story and identity of Mr. X remains untold.

52
Bring the Kids Along

As I left a donor's house, I encountered one of her sons in the driveway. He had just arrived from his home in another town. We were acquainted and he no doubt knew why I was there visiting his widowed mother. She had established an endowment in her husband's name and was also a fairly generous donor to the annual fund. Most recently she had given $10,000 for a gift annuity.

As we briefly exchanged greetings, I sensed tension in the air. I felt he was upset with me for coming to see his mother on behalf of the university (his alma mater). Did he resent losing a portion of his expected inheritance? Did he feel I was being too pushy with his mother?

Though this incident occurred several years ago, the feelings linger. They remind me of the importance of bringing the kids along when the parent(s) make a gift, or at least trying our best not to antagonize them. Some feel very possessive of their parent's wealth, while others respect their parents' wishes and understand their own lack of ownership. Still, it can be tricky to keep everyone feeling positive about a gift.

The next time I saw the donor's son, I extolled his mother and expressed appreciation for her generosity. While careful not to divulge new information, I expanded the appreciation to include him. I tried to bring him along, but I fear I failed.

53
The Enriching Effect of Planned Giving

I've been helping a local organization expand their planned giving program. We've gone through the process of developing an endowment program and are currently awaiting word from the State Insurance Commissioner regarding our application to issue gift annuities.

As part of the expansion process, I provided the board with a draft of an investment policy for their consideration. After all, they'd better get ready to steward the resources that will eventually come under their control. Also, having a sound policy in place is valuable when a discriminating donor inquires about such things.

After reviewing the document, the board decided to call a less formal meeting for those who wanted to talk further about the matter. Eight members came. One member admitted she was uncomfortable in that she didn't understand some of the terms and ideas of the nine-page document. "I don't want to approve something I don't thoroughly understand," she said. Another person asked a thoughtful question about a point on page two. Another offered some thoughts on an item on page four.

For nearly two hours the board members asked questions, offered suggestions and discussed issues. In the end, they unanimously agreed to recommend acceptance by the full board. Even the member who had earlier expressed discomfort with her lack of knowledge offered support.

Driving back to my office, it hit me: Planned giving was forcing these people to deepen their understanding of financial issues and enlarge their commitment to be informed board members. A planned giving program does that! The issues and aspects of running a healthy planned giving program tend to enrich the involvement of those who hold ultimate responsibility for the organization.

The board's quest for understanding is further demonstrated by the administrator's request that I conduct three two-hour sessions for the development staff and the board of directors on the subject of charitable gift planning. We start next week.

54

The Puzzle

I had been complaining that a recently completed 1,000-piece puzzle lacked a level of difficulty appropriate to my expertise. My daughter, seizing the opportunity, presented me with a gift-wrapped box of 2,500 pieces of hook-and-eye cardboard. "Here's a challenge for ya, Dad. Good luck."

The picture on the box drew me in. Snow-clad mountains against a deep blue sky. A broken-down barn and shed with varied shades of brown. Lots of grayish fencing, strands of barbed wire, many shadowy areas and several grasses.

The pieces appeared unusually small and remarkably similar in shape. For example, I found it easy to line up 20 pieces of solid blue sky with no apparent difference in shape. Only when I connected two pieces and turned them over could I tell whether they were a perfect fit. Yes, this puzzle presented a challenge.

During an entire week of vacation I worked on the puzzle. At times my wife joined me and we'd sit at the dining room table for hours without talking, just staring at the little fragments. Occasionally, one of us would pick up a piece and consult the cover of the box for clues.

I fetched a dozen or so gift-box lids and began to sort similar colors into each box. "All it takes is a little organization," I told the family.

My wife spent less and less time at the table. The kids dropped out totally after the second day. I was on my own: just me and the puzzle.

By week's end, and after multiplied hours of intense concentration, only a third of the picture was in place. Still I dogged on. I devoted my evenings and weekends to the "combat zone."

At times my entire family would be sound asleep and there I'd be, hovering over the table trying to find a connection. I arranged the lighting to enhance color and remove glare. I moved around the table to change my perspective.

My wife complained about the unusable table. I saw her eye the empty puzzle box. "Don't you even think about it," I warned. "I'm going to finish this thing if it kills me."

"Maybe we can find a large board to slide it onto so you could work somewhere else."

"No!"

The fun of putting together a colorful puzzle had collapsed. The possibility of failure haunted me. Episodes of frustration occurred repeatedly. Often, I'd leave the table muttering unhappy syllables. My children steered clear.

And then, on a Saturday morning two months after opening the "gift," I came to the dining room with fire in my eyes and sleeves rolled up. More than 1,200 disconnected pieces sneered at me. "This is it!" I said aloud. "I'm not leaving this table until every single piece is in its place!"

Thirty minutes later I stood — a pathetic picture of human wreckage. It was over and I lost. Defeated by little pieces of cardboard.

Whimpering like a whipped dog, I cleared the table. Then, with battered ego, I went in search of my wife to seek understanding and comfort.

Gift planning is like puzzle solving. Pieces of varied color and shape must fit together to complete the gift. Most of the time it comes easy. Sometimes it requires enormous doses of concentration.

And often our satisfaction is directly related to the difficulty of the plan. But some plans just aren't meant to be — like trying to squeeze a square block into a round hole. Impossible plans can sap time and strength and good will. We can lose our perspective as well as our manners.

Oh, for the wisdom to know when to stay at the table and keep working on the puzzle . . . and when to walk away.

55
Try TRUST

Ever had difficulty explaining the workings of a trust to a bewildered prospect? Here's an acrostic that works for me: T R U S T.

The T stands for *Trustor*, the person creating the trust. This is the donor, or couple you are working with. Put them in first place. Expound on your commitment to them as special friends of your organization. Let them know your desire to see them fully satisfied with the gift plan.

The R stands for *Recipients*, those who benefit from the trust. These are the beneficiaries of the trustor's generosity. As you know, there are two categories: the income recipient(s) and the remainder recipient(s). The charity can receive either income or remainder, depending on the nature of the trust. In the interest of full disclosure, you can point out the possibility of multiple remaindermen.

The U stands for *Understandings*, the written agreement. A collection of instructions and requirements. You can also refer to the federal and state laws as an umbrella set of understandings. Talk about irrevocability and the importance of getting the document done right. Express your commitment to help them understand the understandings. Stress the value of independent counsel.

The S stands for *Substance*, the assets placed into the trust. (You could also use the less formal term, stuff.) Here's where you talk about appropriate and inappropriate assets, and the sequence of getting the substance into the trust. Valuation issues fit in nicely here.

The final letter, T, stands for *Trustee*, the person or corporation who oversees the trust. The trustee is legally responsible for making sure that the understandings in the trust document are prudently honored under the umbrella of all applicable state and federal laws. Talk about the pros and cons of various trustee possibilities.

I know this little dissertation is pabulum for 99 percent of you. But the outline just may come in handy sometime when you are trying to communicate to the uninformed.

56
Where to Put Anger

I once worked for a boss, now deceased, who used to anger me so much I'd spit railroad spikes. Several times during my employment under him I got so riled I sat down at the typewriter and pounded out a letter to verbally nail him to the wall. I'd thrash him for his insensitivity and pommel him for making my life difficult. When I finished, you could see steam rising from the paper.

I'd seal the oracle in an envelope and label it CONFIDENTIAL and PERSONAL. Then I'd march down to his office (after hours), let myself in and place the letter on his desk — smack in the middle. Then I'd go home.

Usually about 2 AM, I'd wake in a cold sweat. *Oh dear, what if he actually reads that letter? I was too harsh, too mean. Better go and get it.* So I'd get up and drive to his office. Whew! I was always relieved to see the letter still laying there. I'd grab it and get out of there pronto. Then I'd go back to bed and sleep like a log.

I went through this little ritual several times during a 10-year period. Always, I fully intended to "give him a piece of my mind." And, always, I was relieved to retrieve the letter. (Why didn't I wise up and use invisible ink?)

Now, of course, there's a time and place to sit down with your boss and talk about difficulties in the workplace. Communication problems need to be confronted. But not when you're seething inside.

Better to explode on paper and cool off overnight before talking with your boss. You might even find, as I did, that simply "spilling your guts in a letter" is enough therapy to reduce or even eliminate the need to pursue the matter further.

57
Surprises at the Door

A PGO colleague of mine went to the door of a prospect, an elderly woman who was blind. When she opened the door, my friend noted she was wearing a sheer blouse. Obviously, she was unaware that her privacy was being compromised. With his eyes steadfastly locked on her face, he conducted the visit hastily at the doorway and then bid her farewell . . . wondering what she would later think should she discover her revealing attire.

I was told of another PGO who knocked on the door of a new

prospect only to be confronted, when the door opened, by a woman without a nose. Caught off guard by the strange sight, the visitor's chin dropped to the floor and his eyeballs lunged forward to focus on the place of the missing appendage. An awkward moment ensued. Then, in a gallant effort to redeem the moment, he said, "Does that cause you any pain?" A pleasant visit followed, but the poor PGO confesses an ongoing uneasiness when he rings the bell at the door of a new prospect.

58
Serendipity Gifts

I'm always amazed at the way some gifts pop up out of nowhere. For example, take the couple who drove by the campus every day. They knew nothing about the school, except what they saw from their car window. Over time, the buildings and grounds and students affected them. They liked what they saw.

One day the president's phone rang and the couple offered to make a major, non-cash contribution. No letter of appeal, no cultivation visits, no tricky strategies — just a gift out of the blue.

I recall an 84-year-old widower who involved his professional advisor in an on-site inspection of regional colleges and universities. They visited several campuses to determine where he would leave his estate. The word eventually came that we had been selected as one of four schools to receive his wealth. Nice surprise.

Or take the city bus driver who occasionally wandered into the student union building. The end of his route landed him at the campus and so he'd take advantage of the time and place to get a cup of coffee.

One day an elderly friend of his who lived across town asked his advice concerning the disposition of her estate. He told her about the university and the quality of students he had observed.

"Why not leave it there?" he suggested. She followed his advice and we were invited into the planning picture.

Such unsolicited gifts tell us not to take our well-crafted marketing plans too seriously. They also teach us that people out there are watching us and appraising our value. Pleasant surroundings, a worthy mission, obvious results and a good reputation do their part to produce an ongoing supply of serendipity gifts.

59
All-Day Suckers

Monkey see, monkey do. That's what happened to me years ago when I started to receive notes from a thoughtful colleague. When I gave a talk or published an article or did something else unusual, this person took the time to send a note of appreciation. And not to me only. I learned from others that he did the same thing to them. Over the years he had cultivated the habit of sending notes to express an uplifting thought.

When I became a planned giving officer I tried to adopt the note idea. I obtained some nicely printed fold-over note stationery on colored card stock, with matching envelopes. At first, I carried a supply with me and jotted notes as people came to mind. Just simple "Thinking of You" kind of notes. Then I passed them to my secretary and asked her to type the name and address on the envelopes and mail them.

Before long, I began to forget who I sent cards to and who I neglected. This led to the following plan. We identified the birthdays for all our trustors, annuitants and others who had made a deferred gift to our institution. At the first of the month, my secretary prepared the envelopes (typed) and placed the cards on my desk for signing. I added a note and signed my first name and passed it back for her to mail at the appropriate time.

At the halfway mark between birthdays, she also prepared one of the note cards for my notation and signature. So twice a year, each person would get two personalized notes from me. Occasionally, I'd send additional notes when I became aware of illness or other special circumstances.

Each month, my secretary gave me a list of all the birthdays for that month and the persons who were midway between birthdays. I put a copy on my desk and one in my car. Sometimes I'd pick up the phone and call someone on their birthday as an added personal touch.

I always hand-wrote the notes which sent a message in and of itself. Sometimes I even wrote out the address on the envelope. And when my secretary did the addresses, she typed them so her handwriting would not clash with mine inside the note.

I also used the note cards to build bridges among the faculty and staff. I programmed myself to do at least one per day, using the staff phone directory as a guide and checking off the names I covered.

The notes were short and sweet. Something positive, like, "I appreciate the good things you do every day to make this a better place. Thanks for being here."

Cards and notes are worth far more than the time and minor expense they entail. They create fertile ground for growing positive relationships. The goodwill pays off when people get ready to give.

Phone calls are good, but personal notes are better. They are tangible expressions, something the recipient can refer to again and again. Phone calls are jelly beans; personal notes are all-day suckers.

In the last nine months I've received no less than three notes of kindness and encouragement from the person I referred to earlier. Though he's a busy and successful professional living in Kentucky, he still maintains his note-writing habit. He's still passing out all-day suckers.

60
Today!

You sneeze. Your nose runs. You feel tired and achy. The symptoms and sufferings are so universal we refer to the condition as the "common" cold.

"Drink lots of liquid, get plenty of rest, take two aspirin. Oh yes, chicken soup seems to help."

But common as the cold is, there's another malady that afflicts us even more frequently. Symptoms include compound laziness, multiple excuses and the incessant use of the term, "tomorrow." I refer, of course, to the ailment known as procrastination.

"I'll phone those annuitants — tomorrow."
"I'll be more considerate of my staff — tomorrow."
"I'll visit those prospects — tomorrow."
"I'll do that report — tomorrow."
"I'll draft that letter — tomorrow."
"I'll read that newsletter — tomorrow."

Procrastination is subtle. Sneaky. Before we know it, opportunities vanish and we stand staring into the sunset.

An advertising slogan says, "Today is the first day of the rest of your life." That's right — today, not tomorrow. Tomorrow's illusive. It's always out there making big claims for itself. But it never really comes. Every day is "today." We are born, we live and we die — today. Today is all we have.

We can plan for the future. We can look forward to tomorrow. But we can only live today. Whatever we do, we must do today.

So shake off "later-itis." Grab hold of today. Seize your opportunities. Go get 'em — today!

Okay, okay, so how do we do it?

Make a list. Do it first thing in the morning. Identify the things you will accomplish during the day. Make it reasonable. Listing 400 things will only cause frustration.

Rank your list. Instead of beginning with the easy stuff, start right out with the hard ones. Do them first and the rest of the day will be downhill.

Reward yourself. Checking off a finished project can bring satisfaction. I've been known to add things to my list that I'd already done, just to have the pleasure of checking them off. When you finish, do something you enjoy. Pamper yourself.

King Solomon used the term, "sluggard," to describe the procrastinators of his day. The word still fits. Consider the slug the next time you feel like saying, "tomorrow."

The wise king had a better way to face the day: "Whatever your hand finds to do, do it with all your might, for in the grave, where you are going, there is neither working nor planning nor knowledge nor wisdom."

What if you fail to complete your daily "do list"? Should you stick your head in a meat grinder? Don't be too hard on yourself. After all, if you always accomplish your daily goals, you're probably reaching too low. Better to try and fail than to fail to try. Be forgiving.

I've put off writing this little article too long. This morning I determined to do it today. And I did!

61
The Receipt Connection

I don't know who came up with the idea, but it was a winner. Our development office began to flag any gift of $100 or more that came to the university. The receipts were prepared and envelopes typed. Then they were sent to those of us who worked on the front lines. We also received a computer printout of each donor's giving record.

Any receipt that involved a planned giving donor or prospect came to me. (My prospects had been predetermined by various methods and assigned to me on the master computer.) When I received the receipts, I sorted them into three piles: notes, calls, visits. The receipts in the note pile received a handwritten message of thanks. I'd often add a personal note as well. I recorded on the printout that I had sent the personalized receipt.

The call pile received a phone call, at least an attempted call (the number was on the printout). I thanked them for their gift and expressed interest in their family and activities. Notes of the conversation were jotted on the printout and sent to the data entry person for recording.

The third pile was reserved for larger gifts or for persons I was actively cultivating. They became part of my visitation schedule. Delivering the receipt personally gave me a wonderful means of expressing gratitude and talking about the university.

If I couldn't reach them because of schedule or distance, I'd phone them and/or dictate a letter to accompany the receipt.

The receipt connection went like clockwork. It was a point of reference, a connecting link. Not only was I able to keep up-to-date on the giving activity of "my" donors, I was able to use their generosity as a means to further the cultivation process.

62
Just Horsin' Around

"When I get to L.A.," I said, "I'll need a rental car. Get me a compact; something inexpensive." A few days later, I received the plane tickets and car reservation form.

I was going to Southern California in mid-March to speak to the Planned Giving Council of Ventura County — about 80 miles northwest of L.A. When I arrived at LAX, I went out to the curb to find a van that would take me to the car rental lot. Finally, a van arrived and I hopped in and off we went.

"We don't seem to have a compact in stock right now," I was told. "How about an upgrade?"

Through the window, my eye fastened on a brand new Mustang convertible. "How much is the convertible?"

The quote rocked me back and I asked him to keep looking for a compact. After all, I explained, my reservation form indicated I had been promised a compact.

The representative went out to the lot to have a firsthand look for a compact car. He returned shaking his head.

"How about making me a deal on the Mustang?" I asked.

"How much?"

I quoted a ridiculously low price. He said, "Okay."

And so off I drove, top down, in my hot little Mustang for a hair-blowing trip up and down the freeways of L.A. A rain-soaked Seattle family man in his mid-fifties, speeding along, sunglasses in place, listening to surround-sound speakers blaring cruis'n music. Is this living or what?

After a night cramming for my two presentations, I met my host at his office in Camarillo. Then we headed to the restaurant for the 10:30 pre-luncheon workshop. A nice group of about 35 persons showed up. "The biggest group we've had in two years," I was told. Somebody from Santa Barbara. A person or two from Oxnard. Several from Ventura. Someone from Thousand Oaks. Several from Camarillo. A pleasant group of people brought together by their common involvement in planned giving.

My assigned topic was "Plugging Your Board Into Your Planned Giving Program." After my host pumped up the audience with a generous though undeserved introduction, I launched into my presentation and a mound of overheads. As the workshop progressed, I was pleased to find several board members in the audience. It underscored my point that these planned giving training events are excellent opportunities to educate and inspire board members . . . who can then pass along their understandings and enthusiasm to the larger board.

At noon we broke for a buffet lunch. Several newcomers arrived. After the meal and accompanying conversation, the council president strode to the podium for some routine council business.

And then I got my second crack at the crowd. My topic: "The Amazing GANIMŪCRUT Gift Plan" — something about combining a gift annuity and net-income-with-make-up charitable remainder unitrust.

Other planned giving councils provide a pre-lunch workshop with their regular luncheon meeting, but this was my first time to experience it. I was impressed and found myself wondering why every council doesn't adopt this two-part meeting plan. I was also impressed with the healthy mixture of for-profit and nonprofit gift planners.

I finished at 1:30 p.m. After the room emptied, I had some further conversation with my host. Then I swung into the saddle and galloped my wild Mustang back onto the freeway for another look-at-me-I'm-so-cool ride.

Naturally, I took the long way to L.A. — down through Malibu Canyon and along the coast. Just me and my horse.

Well . . . all good things must end and I soon found myself back at the barn, handing over the reins of my lathered Mustang.

Two days of California sun. Two days of hobnobbing with positive people. Two days of ridin' the open trail. Two days of reminding myself: "I love this job!"

63

The Big Picture

The sun gives light and warmth. The soil gives grain and flower. The sea yields food and moisture. The earth gives oil and mineral. Clouds give rain. Trees give oxygen. Bees give honey. Birds give song. The whole world, it seems, is one gigantic system of giving. A vast network of repeated gifts.

Seen in this light, we might look upon our non-giving or small-giving constituents as discordant members of the natural order. Further, we might view our job, as gift planners, as healers seeking to help nongivers discover the healthy, wholesome benefits of giving . . . seeking to bring harmony with the givingness that surrounds.

To put it another way, our Creator has endowed us with the capacity to plan and to give. Consequently, we are more complete when we give purposefully and generously of our time, our talents and our treasure.

And we gift planners are blessed when we encourage and enable others to give.

64
Name Dropping

I have a new friend who's a planned giving officer in central Florida. We had breakfast together in Orlando. Though we had corresponded, this was our first face-to-face meeting.

We entered a coffee shop where I had eaten breakfast the previous morning. The same waitress came to take our order. She had a name tag pinned to her blouse. I had seen it before, but ignored it in my thoughts.

My friend saw the tag and addressed her by name. Three or four times during the meal he used her name when she came to our table — not awkwardly or in a silly way, but naturally and sincerely. He treated her as a person. He acted as though she was performing a valuable service.

I detected a change in her demeanor. She smiled more, chatted more amiably and, I think, served us with a bit more flair. She seemed pleased to be waiting on our table. I was embarrassed I had treated her so blandly the day before.

My friend also used my name throughout our conversation. Sometimes when people do this to me I feel uncomfortable, like they want to sell me a used car or something. But his sincerity eliminated that option. His use of my name made me feel good.

I thought, *This guy does this out of habit. It's part of his manner, his personality.*

The hour ended and we parted company. But the influence of his example remains. It has caused me to examine my attentiveness to the persons I meet and my own use of a person's name.

I read somewhere that the sound of your own name is the sweetest sound in the world. If so, surely it makes sense that we liberally use the name of our donors and prospects in our conversations with them. Using it will remind us that we are talking to a person (not a gift source) and it will let them know that they, individually, are important to us. We may not be able to get their name on a building or endowment fund, but we can, by naming them often, honor them and acknowledge their worth.

Would it be wise to weave a person's name, genuinely, into the conversation at least three times during every visit? I think so. Over time it might even become a habit. And my guess is that such a habit would immeasurably enhance our interpersonal skills . . . and our successes as gift planners.

65
On Rearing Philanthropists

Last week I attended a presentation on philanthropy. One of the notes I scribbled on my pad relates to the speaker's emphasis on "learned philanthropy." "Philanthropy," he said, "is not in our genes; it's a learned behavior. You don't come into the world with an appetite for giving; you learn it from observation and experience." Philanthropy is a taste we develop, a habit we acquire.

Just because a person is mature in his or her ability to make money doesn't mean that the same person is an adult when it comes to giving. Our society is rife with folks who never caught the spirit nor learned the blessings of philanthropy. They are charitable infants.

Our challenge as gift planners is to turn these youngsters into philanthropic adults. And one way to do this, according to the speaker, is to get people involved in a charity by first convincing them of the economic benefits of a particular gift plan. Once they invest in the cause, they will be more likely to draw near to it and develop the kind of ties that promote philanthropic understanding and involvement. In other words, a person's heart will follow his or her financial commitments.

66
Take This Outline, Please

I made a little presentation the other day touting the benefits of charitable gift annuities. Since you were unable to attend, I thought you might appreciate having a look-see at my overhead transparency. And so, by popular demand, here it is for your reading pleasure. Feel free to enjoy it, frame it, write a song about it, use it, share it with your relatives . . . whatever.

1. *Income Enhancer.* Many older donors find that a current payment gift annuity provides more income than some of their other assets. They like those 9, 10 or even 11 percent payment rates.

2. *Retirement Supplier.* Some of the younger donors are looking at deferred payment gift annuities as a means to supplement their retirement program. By obtaining a deferred gift annuity each year, they receive a nice tax deduction and store up needed income for their retirement years.

3. *Family Provider.* Gift annuities can be used to provide for spouses, older parents and physically challenged children. A gift annuity lets you make a gift to a worthy charity and a gift of lifetime income to a loved one. This can be accomplished with a current payment gift annuity, a deferred payment gift annuity or, at death, with a testamentary gift annuity.

4. *Tax Reliever.* A gift annuity created during life produces a charitable income tax deduction. A gift annuity created at death provides an estate tax deduction. Also, annuity payments received during one's life expectancy are partially tax-free. As always, tax benefits and possible liabilities should be discussed with a qualified professional advisor.

5. *Legacy Producer.* Gift annuities are often paired with an endowment program. A portion of the charitable gift amount can be earmarked to create a new endowment fund (perhaps in the donor's name) or enhance another endowment already in existence.

So there you have it — one of the finest presentation outlines ever to enter the kingdom of gift-planningdom. Take it . . . please.

OK, OK, so I didn't include the *home retainer* (remainder in home) or the *education funder* (college annuity option) or even the *stepped annuity* arrangement. Nor did I talk about the partial bypass of capital gains or the enjoyment of membership in a heritage society. Looks like I forgot a lot of stuff!

Oh well, five points are easier to remember.

67
Trusts and Trust

We drove to the bank so they could sign the unitrust documents in front of a notary. As we walked back to the car, I thanked them profusely and affirmed their decision. "This is tremendous," I effused. "You're going to be more and more glad you did this as the years go by."

"I hope so," she said, expressing a bit of apprehension. After all, it was her husband who had been so enthusiastic about the plan. He had been the driving force.

The process had taken 18 months and had included the education of a CPA and the toleration of a fee-driven attorney. But, finally, it came together.

As I held the car door open, I encouraged her further: "I think you've done a really good thing. You'll see; it's going to work out just fine."

She looked up at me as I started to close the door and said something that still rings in my ears: "Roger, I trust you."

Isn't that what it so often comes down to? After all the words have been said, all the explanations provided, all the professional advice offered — anxious donors place their trust in the planned giving officer, the one who developed a relationship with them and who walked with them through the entire process. This trust is heavy-duty stuff.

68
Setting the Tone

I've learned, as you have, that preparing for a successful visit includes more than gathering data about the prospective donor. Or more than rehearsing a case statement about your organization. A good visit requires emotional as well as mental preparation.

If I go to see someone and I'm burdened with work or home pressures, the visit suffers. I may have chalked up another visitation credit, but I certainly didn't make the best impression for my organization. It's possible some visits might even be considered counter-productive.

Things go much better when I'm in an upbeat mood. So, to help put myself into a positive frame of mind, I developed a little checklist to run through before knocking on the door. These seven affirmations seem to help.

No. 1 — *I will be cheerful and positive.*

No. 2 — *I will compliment them on the good I observe.*

No. 3 — I will bombard them with words of appreciation.
No. 4 — I will listen attentively and reinforce their positive remarks.
No. 5 — I will be confident and enthusiastic about my organization.
No. 6 — I will offer them the opportunity to make a difference.
No. 7 — I will leave them thanking me for stopping by.

If I go into a visit intent on leaving the donor prospect in a happy state of mind, I find myself acting in ways to engender that result. A good visit should produce good feelings, good will and expressions of appreciation. And a good gift!

69

Planned Giving at Home

Early in December our family begins to lay plans to give a Christmas basket to a special family. This practice has become an annual event with us, though the recipient family changes.

The tradition began more than a decade ago when our family received such a gift from another family. It made us feel so good we decided to extend the blessing to others.

Our gift-planning process follows the same pattern year after year. The six of us put aside some money and talk about what we should put in the basket.

Then the big day arrives and we pile in the car to go shopping for the basket and the goodies. We visit two or three stores before it's over. We gather fruit, nuts, cheeses, jams, crackers, cookies, candies and gourmet delicacies of every description. If it's good or fun to eat, we get it. We opt for things a family would not normally buy for themselves.

Loading the oversized basket is a joint project. We jam every item into the container (gift vehicle). Then we wrap the whole thing in brilliant colored paper and place a big ribbon on top. We each write a brief message in a card which we tape to the paper.

On Christmas Eve we drive to the unsuspecting family, quietly mount the stairs and ring the bell. When the door opens we sing, "We wish you a Merry Christmas, We wish you a . . ." Then my son carries the 50-pound basket into the house and sets it on the table. With that, we depart.

Who gets the most out of the gift? We hear reports of excitement and enjoyment. But the happiness of the receivers is overshadowed by the joys we experience in planning and delivering the gift. And, as the primary enabler of the gift, I think I receive the biggest bang of all. Making the gift happen is downright fun.

This is one reason I like the profession of planned giving. There's nothing quite so satisfying as working alongside giving-minded persons to enable them to make gifts to the charities they love. It's like orchestrating Christmas baskets all year long.

70
Good Intentions

I have used, for some time, a device to help smooth the way for a completed gift. I call it a "Letter of Intent." After talking through a gift illustration with prospective donors, and gaining their acceptance, I go back to my office and prepare a one-two page statement containing all of the relevant items regarding the establishment of the gift plan. I include birthdates and social security numbers. I make it in the form of a letter to the charity from the donors and provide a place where each spouse can sign and date the letter.

For unitrusts, I include the percentage amount, the type of unitrust, the frequency of payments, the remainder beneficiaries and percentages — all the particulars an attorney would need to draft the document.

If funded with real estate, I include a description of the property and understandings about providing an environmental audit and qualified appraisal. The letter also indicates that "we understand the importance and value of consulting with our own professional advisors before signing any legal document."

The donors acknowledge in the letter that they understand it to be non-binding and that they are providing notice of their intentions in order to ensure good communication and to help the charity/trustee assess the assets and terms of the proposed gift.

I prepare two copies of the Letter of Intent, one for the donors and the other for the charity. If possible, I deliver these in person and go over each paragraph thoroughly with the donors to make sure they fully understand the meaning and import of the words. I make clear that I do not want to put words in their mouths, but rather to reflect the true expressions of their gift intentions.

I encourage them to reflect on the letter for a few days and to share it with their advisors. My goal is to make sure we are all starting off in the same direction. Several revisions may be warranted before everyone agrees.

Once signed, the letter becomes the centerpiece in discussions among the gift acceptance committee and serves as a guide in the drafting of documents. It is something concrete, a substantial record representing positive progress in the planned giving program.

I have also found that once the donors have signed the Letter of Intent, they find it easier to sign the final documents when that time arrives. Indeed, everything seems to go smoother after the donors state their specific intentions in writing.

Not all Letters of Intent result in completed gifts. I am even now smarting over a proposed gift that failed to materialize. But maybe, just maybe, having gone through the process of stating and signing their intentions, the prospective donors will revisit the idea at a later time. Without hounding them, I will let them know that we continue to value their friendship and support.

71
Appetizing Alternatives

The 40-something couple had a debt-free, 10-acre piece of appreciated land and they wanted to sell it and make an outright gift with a portion of the proceeds. When they approached someone in the charity's finance department about their plan, the person, being alert, suggested they talk to me.

A few days later I was sipping coffee at their kitchen table, listening to a description of the land and their plans to sell it in order to obtain cash to pay down their house mortgage, cover the taxes and give $100,000 to their favorite charity. The undeveloped land, with a view, was perfect as a suburban home site with enough land for a couple of horses. Similar parcels were going for $250,000.

As they talked, I learned about their other assets, their two businesses and the fact they were doing quite well financially. Obviously, they could afford to make an irrevocable gift of this size.

When my turn came, you know exactly what I said. After commending them for their generous intentions, I pointed out the difference in making a gift of this sort before and after the sale. Using my yellow pad, I showed how they could save capital gain taxes by giving an undivided interest in the land prior to the sale. They grasped my point immediately. (I also explained the difference between a cash gift and a gift of appreciated property in terms of the 50 and 30 percent levels of deductibility.)

Then I asked, "Would you be interested in looking at another option, something that would meet your objectives of a current gift and a smaller mortgage, as well as permit you to escape taxes on all of the capital gain, yield a larger tax deduction, allow you to make an even larger gift and provide a built-in retirement plan?" He said, "Go for it."

Again, you know what I said: I presented the wonders of a charitable remainder unitrust. I suggested they consider splitting their gift as before, but instead of keeping the non-gift portion, they would use that part to fund a 5 percent charitable remainder unitrust with the full remainder going to the charity.

I diagrammed the scenario, showing how they could bypass capital gain, obtain a charitable tax deduction, reduce the size of their estate, obtain tax-free build-up inside the trust and establish a nice retirement fund that would likely provide them a healthy quarterly supplement by the time they reached age 65. I also gave them a rough estimate of what would eventually go to the charity at the end of the trust.

I suggested they could apply the income from the trust against their current mortgage. Later, they could use it to help fund their children's college education. And yes, I mentioned the possibility of replacing the value of the asset with a wealth-replacement life insurance trust.

Encouraged by their obvious interest in the unitrust plan, I quickly ticked through some of the optional features in the interest of full disclosure. I noted they could reserve the right to change or add charities and even switch the trustee. I explained the differences between a standard, net-income and net-income-with-make-up trust and why the charity (trustee) would require the second type.

I mentioned the option of selecting a higher payout percentage but explained the advantages of the lower percentage for them and the charity. I said the charity might be willing, under certain conditions, to administer the trust without a fee.

Normally, I restrain myself from dumping so much information during a first visit, but these folks were mentally sharp and inquisitive. They were hungry for information. So I babbled on.

I told them about the giving process, including the qualified appraisal and a possible environmental audit. I even advanced the idea that they might consider adding some cash to the trust to cover taxes and other expenses if the property was slow in selling.

I concluded by offering to return with a computerized illustration of the gift plan, including the variations I had related. "I'll go through the whole thing slower and with more detail," I said.

"And, if you want, I'll meet with your accountant." Two hours after I arrived, they walked me to the door, enthusiastic about our time together. They promised to call me after talking over these new ideas.

What had once seemed like a simple, open-and-shut case of selling a piece of property and making a gift had turned into a fascinating exploration of several possibilities. Along with their coffee, they got an appetizing taste of the pleasures of charitable gift planning. I think they'll make a meal of it.

72
Procedures, Procedures

I had come to this electronics store a year ago for a $2 item. I remember being annoyed when the salesman quizzed me at the checkout counter about my name, address and phone number. He entered this in the computer so they could send me sale announcements.

Now here I was again. When I opened the door, a salesman pounced on me from 20 feet away. *He should be at the used car lot down the street*, I thought.

"What can I help you with?" he gushed.

"I'm looking for a 25-foot extension cord for my stereo headphones."

"I've got just what you need." He went and took a package from the shelf and led me to the counter.

Placing his hands on the computer keyboard, he asked, "What are the last four digits of your phone number?"

I placed a $20 bill on the counter. "I don't want to go through all of this. I just want to buy the cord."

"It won't take long. It's something I need to do."

"How much is the cord? I've got the money right here. Can't you just make change and let it go at that?"

"Hey, my job's on the line here. Just give me your last four numbers and I'll call up your name. You're probably in the computer anyway."

I surrendered. "My home number ends with 7038."

The screen came up empty. "They clear the records every so often; when did you say you were in here last?"

"About a year ago . . . and I had to do this whole song and dance then — even though I'd been in here a year before that."

"Well, it will only take a sec. What's your last name?"

"Really, I'm telling you, I don't want to go through this. Can't I just buy this cord?"

He began entering something in the computer so I asked what he was doing.

"I've got to fill out something anyway . . . it will take just as long."

I complained again. "I don't know who in management came up with this procedure, but I can tell you it doesn't endear me to your store. It's like you won't sell me anything unless I divulge personal information."

A nearby customer looked at me with a face that said: *You're a fruitcake, fella. Why don't you just go with the program and give the guy your name?*

Completing his computer work (without my assistance), the frustrated salesman took my money and made change, which he handed me along with a sack containing the cord. I left.

Today I've been thinking about that little episode . . . and recalling a time or two when I, as a planned giving officer, threw cold water on a prospective donor by trying to squeeze the person through a meaningless procedure devised by a bean counter in the back room. Instead of exuding a can-do attitude, I donned a furrowed brow and wrestled with the dissonance I felt between the desires of the donor and a requirement in the manual.

Painful memories. Would that I had issued warm fuzzies at the proposal of the gift and come back later with thoughtful, tactful reasons on how such a great gift could be made better. Too soon old, too late smart.

73
A Little Help From Our Friends

I gave a presentation to the advancement committee of an educational institution extolling the virtues of an aggressive planned giving program. One of the 15 attendees, a friend of mine, is a fund-raising consultant who serves on the committee as a volunteer. In fact, he had something to do with my presence there as a presenter.

Later that evening I called my friend at his home to get his feedback on my presentation. He said nice things. I went to bed feeling good about myself.

The next day my friend called me back. "I've been thinking about your presentation," he said, "and I want to give you some additional feedback."

"Go ahead," I responded, uneasiness swelling within.

Starting with affirming words, he went on to comment on my voice level and my need to use more tonal variation during my presentation. He also said I needed to avoid slowing down my speech at the end of a thought as I formulate my next sentence.

Even though he expressed himself carefully, sprinkling his comments with affirming phrases, my defenses wasted no time running to their battle stations. I wanted to excuse myself, to argue, to justify. But I bit my tongue.

I instructed myself to recognize his sincere and tactful approach. *He's right,* I thought, *I do need to improve in these areas. This is constructive criticism and it's good. I should be glad he cares enough about my success to say these things.*

This little experience in professional growth has reminded me of the need I have — we have — for honest and affirming feedback from our peers. The next time you give a presentation, why not engage a colleague to provide constructive criticism? How about taking a colleague on your next round of visits and follow up with a feedback session? How about inviting a peer to critique a manuscript before it sees publication?

If you decide to enlist the assistance of a colleague in sharpening your skills, you can help by making it easy for that person to point out areas of weakness. You can listen without defending yourself. You can express sincere appreciation. You can even offer to return the service if desired.

With a little help from our friends, we can become better gift planners and do more for the causes we represent.

74
When Gift Planners Collide

What do you do when you discover you and a planned giving officer from another organization are working with the same donor? And what if you are both making major deferred gift proposals? And what if the other person is promoting things you don't agree with? And what if you sense a spirit of competition in the wind?

"These are the times that try men's souls." And women's souls. Such occasions call for every ounce of discernment and tact you can muster. What you do can spell the difference between a tragedy for everyone and an arrangement yielding mutual satisfaction.

It seems to me you have at least three options: 1. Ignore the "competition" and go right on doing your own thing. 2. Contact the other planned giving officer and establish a line of communication and, perhaps, coordination. 3. Talk with the donor and let his or her wishes guide you concerning your involvement with the other PGO.

In reviewing my own experience, I find I have chosen all three options, depending on any number of variables. My decision seems to depend on the age and personality of the donor; the depth of my own involvement with the donor; the size and complexity of the gift; my relationship with the other planned giving officer; the PGO's level of flexibility, fairmindedness and integrity; and my own stress quotient.

At my best, I attempt to follow the golden rule of planned giving: "Do unto the donor what you would do were the donor your mother." I try to put the donor first and the organization I represent second. But this can be tricky if those at the home office, unacquainted with the delicacies involved, turn up the heat for an aggressive, get-the-gift-no-matter-what approach.

Sometimes I wish we had a professional guidebook that provided a "Here's How to Act" list for every occasion, a sort of Emily Post manual for PGOs. Such a book could address the various ethical issues, as well as provide practical guidance for handling any number of problematic situations. Oh, give me this book.

75
Hourly Professionals

Moving from a salaried position as a planned giving officer to the self-employment world of publishing a planned giving newsletter and performing consulting services has taught me something about the dollar value of time. It's helped me better understand the time pressures facing many of the allied professionals who serve as volunteers for various planned giving committees and events. For them, time is money and the time they give to PGOs and charitable organizations may reduce their income. For example, attending a committee meeting during the day could easily cost some of them two or three hundred dollars.

I'm embarrassed to recall the expectations I placed on attorneys and CPAs who were willing to become involved with my planned giving program. I fear I occasionally took advantage of their graciousness and treated them as though they had all the time in the world to give to my cause. Sometimes, when a question arose, I'd grab the phone and call one of my allied professionals for immediate input. I didn't stop to consider the inconvenience this would cause. I now suspect that many of my requests did not justify interrupting them for an answer or advice. I just didn't think about what I was doing.

So, for what it's worth, here are some random suggestions for involving allied professionals. If I were back at my planned giving desk, I'd try to follow these more closely. Begin and end meetings on time. Be prepared with a worthwhile agenda. Make good use of their time. Don't disturb them at their office during the most productive hours — usually mornings. Avoid requesting callbacks; leave messages with a secretary or assistant.

Provide generous and frequent doses of appreciation. Let them know you are trying to be sensitive to their schedule. Don't overinvolve them with multiple assignments. Share materials and useful ideas about planned giving so they are receiving as well as giving. Communicate the mission of your organization and impart something of your own vision and enthusiasm as further justification for their involvement. Help them network with other professionals in the community. In short, make their involvement a positive experience.

76
Out of the Blue

The phone rang today. An elderly gentleman wondered whether I was still helping folks with their planned gifts. I said, "Yes," and then there was a pause. A moment later, on a phone extension, his spouse greeted me.

They told me they had decided to leave all their worldly possessions to an organization I represent. They wanted me to tell them how to do it. I meet with them tomorrow. Sometimes I just want to hug my phone!

77
Charitable Hints

A friend who's a gift-planning accountant in Vancouver, B.C., used the term, "charitable hint," during a conversation in the exhibit area of a regional conference in Seattle. I stopped him: "What was that you said? A charitable hint? What do you mean?"

He explained that a good gift planner listens for subtle hints in talking with prospective donors. These hints may lead to planned gifts. For example, when people with appreciated property say, "We can't afford to give to your cause," it may simply mean they are property rich and cash poor. A follow-up question might be, "Are you saying you would like to give if you could?" The answer may well lead you into an illustration of a life-income gift.

Another charitable hint might be: "We plan to leave you something in our will." One might be tempted to express gratitude and move on to another prospect. But such a statement hints that they might be willing to consider the advantages of making that future gift now in the form of a charitable remainder trust or gift annuity.

Another hint: "We'd like to help, but we're on a fixed income and it's getting harder and harder to make ends meet." Voila! This might be a marvelous opportunity to introduce these people to the benefits of transferring low-yielding securities into a charitable gift annuity with higher rates.

One more: "Our kids are grown and doing very well." This may hint of less pressure to reserve estate assets for family needs. The folks may be willing to increase their charitable giving. It's worth a follow-up question.

After my conversation with my Canadian friend, I'm listening closer for charitable hints.

78
Think Zoo

We receive a monthly newsletter from the Woodland Park Zoo and Zoological Society. It's an eight-page, fold-over self-mailer. When we got our first issue several years ago, I noticed on the back page (the half page above the mailing label section), a two-inch, one-column boxed "ad" bearing the title, REMEMBER THE ZOO IN YOUR WILL.

Under the title I read something like, "Your deferred gift can be a lasting memory by helping build the zoo for future generations. Bequests should be made to the Woodland Park Zoological Society . . . ." And then followed a phone number for further information.

I remember being impressed with the stark simplicity of the "ad." No clip art, no fancy type, no testimonial — just a box with a standout title and 45 words of text. The next issue of the newsletter carried the same ad. And the next issue. I'm looking at the most recent issue, and there it is again — same ad, same place. To my knowledge, *every* issue includes the ad.

We can spend lots of money on the brochures we send to our mailing list once or twice a year, and big dollars on an occasional display ad. But I suspect the impact of these efforts, while immediately impressive, is short-lived.

It seems to me that the regularity of a simple reminder month after month in the organization's newsletter has a much better chance of establishing an idea in the reader's mind: "When you think of your will, think Zoo." And vice versa: "When you think about the Zoo, consider a bequest."

This kind of marketing is a cost-effective way to build awareness. Every nonprofit out there should be doing this as a bare-minimum effort to encourage planned gifts.

Kudos to Woodland Park Zoo.

79
Jokes Attorneys Tell

One thing about attorneys: They always seem to begin their seminar presentations with a story. As I've listened to these jokes over the years, several things seem apparent. First, the stories are about themselves, about their own profession. Second, the jokes are always a bit sadistic. Third, I hear the same stories over and over. Fourth, the joketellers enjoy themselves. And, fifth, the attorneys laugh the loudest.

In honor of my attorney friends, here's a small collection of well-worn jokes. All of these came from the lips of lawyers.

Joke No. 1: What's the difference between a dead snake and a dead attorney lying on the highway? Skid marks in front of the snake.

Joke No. 2: Three men were stranded on a small island: a banker, a rabbi and a lawyer. Though the mainland was only 100 yards away, the waters churned with hungry sharks. The banker and rabbi refused to swim, fearing for their lives. The attorney stripped down and dove in. Instead of a feeding frenzy, the sharks lined up on two sides, making a path for him. He made it safely to shore.

The rabbi was dumbfounded. "That's incredible," he exclaimed. "How do you explain it?"

Said the banker: "Professional courtesy."

Joke No. 3: "Did you know that they're burying attorneys 10 feet down instead of the usual six feet? You see, down deep they're pretty good people."

Joke No. 4: A lawyer, doctor and minister stood at the bed of a dying man. "I've decided to take my money with me," gasped the man. And then he thrust an envelope into the hand of each professional. "Each envelope contains $100,000," croaked the miser. "At my funeral, place the envelopes in my coffin just before they close the lid." The lawyer, doctor and minister all solemnly promised to follow his last wish.

A few days later, at the funeral, each of the three professionals dutifully dropped their envelope into the casket. Later, after the interment, the three men found themselves riding back to the funeral home in the same car.

The minister was the first to speak. "I just feel terrible. I did something I'm very ashamed of and I need to get it off my chest." With that, he told the other two of his decision to take $30,000 out of the envelope before dropping it into the casket. "We desperately need a new organ at the church and $30,000 will help us meet this need. But I still feel miserable about taking the money."

The doctor spoke next. "I'm glad you told us that, because I also have something to confess. We are raising money for a new wing at the hospital and I took $50,000 out of my envelope before putting it into the casket. I feel terrible."

The attorney was indignant. "Well, I am disgusted! You promised that old man you would put the full amount in the casket. You ought to be ashamed! I want you to know that I took all of the money out of the envelope and exchanged it with a personal check for the *full* amount."

Joke No. 5: A major research university is now using attorneys in their experiments instead of white rats. There are three reasons for this: First, there are more attorneys than white rats. Second, you don't get as attached to attorneys as you do to white rats. And third, quite frankly, there are some things that a rat just won't do.

Joke No. 6: An attorney died and met St. Peter at the Pearly Gates. "Hey, how come I'm here so soon?" complained the lawyer. "I'm only 50 years old. I'm too young to be here." To which St. Peter replied, shuffling through some papers, "Well, according to your time sheets and your billable hours, you're at least 85 years old."

Joke No. 7: What problem do you have with three lawyers buried up to their necks in sand? Not enough sand.

Joke No. 8: What's black, brown and looks good on an attorney? A doberman.

Joke No. 9: How many lawyers does it take to screw in a light bulb? . . .

Hmmmmm . . . I think I'd better stop. After all, I may have trouble finding an attorney if I should need one in the near future.

80
Living 200 Years

People are living longer. At the turn of the century, the average life expectancy was 49 years. In 1990 it was 76 years. According to an article in the *Chicago Tribune*, we can look forward to even longer life spans in the future.

The extensive article by Peter Gorner and Ronald Kotulak reports that researchers are discovering how to extend life. A good diet and appropriate exercise may permit one to live up to 120 years. Another option is to receive periodic "tune-ups" where worn-out growth factors and chemical defense systems are replaced with a younger variety. This could possibly keep the heart ticking for 115 years.

A third possibility is to use drugs and gene therapy to genetically alter the aging process. If this proves feasible, some scientists, according to the article, are predicting life spans "of 200 years and beyond."

Imagine what this would do to our annuity and trust calculations. Instead of 90-year-old singles receiving a high percentage rate for a gift annuity, they would be lucky to get anything. And if a single life span could stretch 200 years, what about a two-life expectancy? One-hundred-and-fifty-year-old George marries 35-year-old Martha and . . .

Think of the struggling nonprofit waiting 135 years for a trust to "mature." And what about the cultivation process? It would last and last and last.

If some donors choose not to receive the life-extending therapy, would we have one set of expectancy tables for them and another for the long livers?

Instead of four score years, we'll be talking 10 score . . . or even more. We'll need warehouses to hold our bulging prospect and donor files. Think of the trust management expenses. Imagine the potential size of a 200-year-old estate!

To keep up with his or her prospects, every planned giving officer will need the genetic treatment. Are you ready for this?

81
Self-Improvement

Copies of the outdated will, a note pad and other papers rested on the table. Sounds from the kitchen revealed the brewing of fresh coffee. The delightful aroma of newly baked pastry filled the air. Ah yes, another planned giving appointment.

Bill and Leora wanted to discuss changes in their estate plan and review some ideas they had for the charity I represented. Mostly, they were interested in bequest possibilities and they wanted my advice about a good attorney. As is my practice, I provided several names for their consideration. We also chatted briefly about trust options, but the small size of their estate and the absence of appreciated property made the bequest option more appropriate at this time. After an hour of thoughtful conversation (and a piece of apple pie ala mode), I bid them good-bye.

Then I did what every good planned giving officer does: I prepared a follow-up letter and wrote a contact report. The report was appropriately circulated and filed. Next, I did something I haven't done in a while, I prepared a "contactor" report. That is, I walked through a personal evaluation of my own behavior during the visit. Not for the brass at the charity, but for me. I wanted to apply some effort toward self-improvement.

How well did I listen to Bill and Leora? How well did I pick up important clues from the surroundings and the conversation? Did I truly seek information from them, or was I mostly interested in what I had to say? How well did I affirm their past involvement with the charity? Did I share new information about the charity and seek to renew their vision of its mission? Was I sincere, genuine, gracious? Did I establish a time or opportunity for another visit? How could I have made the visit better?

The evaluation made me wince. While I found high marks here and there, I also discovered some Cs. Even a D. The exercise made me realize where I need to improve.

I do not have a printed evaluation form to complete following a visit; perhaps I should develop one. After all, professionalism requires earnest efforts at self-improvement.

82
Going for It

This week I will drive to the Lutheran Bible Institute in Issaquah to attend the December meeting of our local planned giving council. It's our first meeting there in several years. Issaquah lies at the east end of Lake Sammamish and is skewered by a strip of concrete known as Interstate 90.

Instead of driving I-90, I'll make the 30-40 minute trip from North Seattle by traveling a curvy road along the north edge of Lake Sammamish. I'll go this way not only for the scenery, but to revisit the route I traveled three years ago when making my way to a meeting of the same council at the same location. It was during the solitude of that trip that the idea of publishing a newsletter for planned giving professionals first entered my mind.

When the thought of a newsletter dawned, I pursued it casually at first, then vigorously. The possibilities intrigued me. Such a publication could unite those of us who labor alone, often misunderstood, in our own institutions. We could reach out and touch each other.

I drove in dream gear, chasing pop-up thoughts with Porsche-like speed. By the time I reached LBI, my mind was doing the Indy 500.

Did I charge into the meeting and announce my entrepreneurial intentions? Not quite. Instead, I opened my umbrella and sloshed to the door. By the time I entered the room, the newsletter fantasy was dead.

Funny how fast some visions fizzle.

I'm not sure when the newsletter idea came back to life. Sometime early in 1990. But this time it took root. By March I had nailed down basic parameters and had run some market tests. I began to play with publication dates and content ideas. A few pre-publication subscriptions trickled in.

Initially, I saw the newsletter as an off-duty pursuit. I could do it in the evenings and on weekends. I'd treat it like a hobby. But the further I went, the more obvious it became that doing the job right would require full-time attention. My earlier years as a professional editor had taught me a thing or two about the demands of publishing a monthly periodical. I knew what lay ahead.

Should I go for it? Or should I walk away? I struggled with the decision.

I considered the burdens of house payments and other major financial commitments. I wrestled with concerns about advancing age and the need for stability and retirement planning. I thought about old dogs and new tricks. And I grappled with my responsibilities as a husband and father of four children — the oldest who was enrolled as a freshman in the university, and who would be able to take advantage of the generous tuition break afforded me as an employee.

My annual contract as director of the university's foundation sat on my desk — adequate salary, generous benefits, great office, abundant resources, good friends. Give it all up for a "paper" dream? Had I lost an oar?

But the calling was too strong, the challenge too compelling. Miss this opportunity and I'd live to regret it.

So with the support of my family, I gave my employer a "pink slip" and, on July 1, 1990, launched my home-based business as a planned giving newsletter publisher.

Was it worth it? Do dogs bark?

83
Seminar in a Cookie

Having finished my rice, meat sauce, greens, dry noodles and other oriental delicacies, I reached for my fortune cookie. Others at my table had already discovered their "fate" and now it was my turn. I broke it and pulled out the little strip of paper. Dim light and small print forced me to lift the paper closer to my half-century-old eyes.

The lights were down because a slide presentation was in progress. A representative of PNC Investment Management and Trust Services was presenting background words to enhance our dining pleasure. He spoke of the economy and the investment of endowment funds.

His presentation was just one of 55 learning opportunities (including repeats) packed into this National Conference on Planned Giving in Pittsburgh, Pennsylvania. It was a classy presentation with slides and attractive. But my mind kept returning to the little piece of paper I had found in my cookie.

It said: "Patience is the way to joy." Hmmmmm. Not a bad thought when applied to planned giving. Patience with donors. Patience with coworkers. Patience with the system. Patience with family members. Patience with yourself. Patience.

Wow! An entire seminar in a cookie!

84
Practicing With Each Other

In early December I travelled to Portland, Oregon, to speak to the Northwest Planned Giving Roundtable. I expected a mere handful to come at such a busy time of the year. Instead, at least 60 gift planners braved the pouring rain to attend — a good portion of the membership. I asked the president how he was able to get such a high percentage of their members to attend a December meeting.

He said that he and others on the executive committee call every member of the council every month to make sure each one knows about the meeting and to urge their attendance. Non-attenders receive special attention.

Additionally, the president makes a point of being there at the outset to shake hands and welcome every planned giving officer and allied professional. I also noticed that during the coffee and conversation period, as well as the after-meeting social time, he "worked the crowd," going from person to person, chatting warmly, introducing people to one another, making sure everyone felt at home.

On the way to the train station, I pushed him for an explanation. He put it like this, "We need to practice with each other what we preach to each other about how to treat our prospects."

85
Table Hopping

The meeting of development officers featured roundtable discussions. When we sat down for lunch, each of us found a colored dot at our place. Half were one color, half another. Except mine — I had a blue dot. When the program began, I learned that my dot identified me as the discussion facilitator for our table.

The first assignment for each table was to go around and make self-introductions. After all eight persons had done this, we addressed the following question: "How did you get into development work?"

Ten minutes later, one half the people at each table went to other tables. They could not sit with someone they sat with previously. Again, after introductions, a question was presented for discussion. This time it was: "What is the single most important quality of a successful development officer?"

After another 10 minutes, the half who had not moved before went to other tables. The third discussion question was: "What is the ideal working situation for a development officer?"

During the program we all met a number of new people and benefitted from a variety of perspectives. One possible improvement (a confessed afterthought of the program leader): encourage each person to bring a supply of business cards. This could help us later to remember who we met.

Next time you schedule roundtable discussions, try the "musical chairs" approach.

86
The Personal Touch

I moderated two 75-minute sessions on "Service and Stewardship" at a National Conference on Planned Giving. Sixty or more gift planners came to each session and most participated in the discussion. We addressed, among other things, the role of a nonprofit in providing recognition to donors following a planned gift. I learned lots from the various speakers.

Some of the participants reported extensive programs of recognition. They treated their donors to certificates, plaques, plants, cards, letters, donor wall designations, special events and other expressions of gratitude. Why do they make so much fuss? Someone offered this reason: "People who are well thanked tend to make repeat gifts."

Others in the room took exception to such elaborate recognition. "Our donors don't want us spending their money on them. They give to further our mission, not to buy plaques or sponsor gratitude gatherings. Furthermore, some of them are adamant about their anonymity."

Most attendees seemed to fall somewhere between these two extremes. They believe something specific should be done to say "thank you," even if it's relatively minor. The biggest complaint was that there isn't enough time to do an adequate job of recognition. After listening to one person recite the elements of their systematic program for recognition, another participant said, "All of these things are well and good, but nothing takes the place of the personal touch." A chorus of heads nodded in harmony.

Whatever comprises a recognition program, people seem to most appreciate a sincere and personal "thank you." Typed letters are good; handwritten notes are better. Cards are good; a phone call is better. A gift sent by mail is good; personal delivery is better. And nothing beats a personal visit in the home. The rule of thumb seems to be, however you say thanks, make it personal.

87
Segment of One

From time to time, *Success* magazine takes a hard look at marketing. A piece on target marketing snagged my attention. The writer pointed out that the really successful companies individualize their marketing strategy. They not only narrow their message to a subgroup of buyers, they tailor their appeals to individuals. They market to a segment of one.

The implications for gift planning appear obvious. If we want to be successful, perhaps we should spend the bulk of our time individualizing our appeals to a handful of prospects rather than pouring money into mailings to the masses. Direct mail has its place, to be sure, but often it can provide a false sense of security that we are doing an adequate job of marketing. It is best used to obtain leads for individualized attention.

Marketing to a segment of one means digging for information about the person through personal interview and office research. It means knowing the individual's interests and involvements, dreams and fears, assets and liabilities. It means spending time with the prospect until there is a bond of respect and trust. It means making that person feel special, important, valued. It means devising a plan that fits like a glove.

Do you have a short list of donor prospects you have identified for individualized attention? If you are successful in this business, my guess is that you have several segments of one.

88
A Piece of the Action

I sat recently at the dining room table with a couple in their 50s. They had confessed very little interest in philanthropy and seemed eager for my help only as it pertained to some of their estate planning questions.

As our conversation neared completion, I asked, "Have you folks ever considered funding an endowment? You know, an ongoing fund that would provide annual financial help to a worthy cause. Something like a yearly scholarship for a needy college student."

"No, no, we're not interested in anything like that. We plan to divide everything with our kids."

It would have been easy to nod and scoot back from the table and thank them for the nice visit. Instead, I said, "Let me tell you what my wife and I did four years ago. After my mother died we wanted to do something to keep her memory alive, something that would remind her grandchildren and great-grandchildren and their children that this woman is part of their history and that she loved music and cared about young people. And so, along with my sister and her husband, we started a little endowment fund at the college we attended. We called it the Mildred M. Schoenhals Music Scholarship Endowment.

"It was easy to set up and we've added to it little by little to where it is now able to produce a modest scholarship for a worthy student."

I told them about the letter we received recently from the young man, a piano student, who was awarded the scholarship and how we stuck that letter on the refrigerator door. I told them of our enjoyment and satisfaction with this ongoing type of gift and how we want someday to increase it with a larger gift from our estate.

By the time I finished they were hooked. He said, "You know, that really sounds like a great idea. I think we might be interested in doing something like that."

How much easier it is to talk to a prospect about making a planned gift when we can give a personal testimony. It doesn't have to be an endowment. What about a deferred gift annuity — even a small one? How about a contribution to the pooled income fund? If nothing else, you could at least add a codicil to your will defining a bequest to your organization. Every planned giving officer can find a way to make a planned gift.

Some people stand on the shore and urge others to venture out and enjoy the water. Others slash out into the water and call back to the planned giving prospects lining the shore: "Come on in! The water's wonderful!"

Postscript
On Your Way in Planned Giving

As a gift planner, you are a philanthropist — with somebody else's money. You build relationships with prospective donors. You plant the seed for a planned gift. You offer options and inspire action. You participate in the process. You enable the gift. And because of all of this, you experience something of the thrill of personally making a major gift to the organization you serve.

You practice this philanthropy again and again. And all the while you are building a circle of loyal and grateful friends who bless you for helping them accomplish something worthwhile. No wonder you find your profession so satisfying, so exciting.

As the years roll by, you accumulate an array of anecdotes and advice. You recall the donors who were motivated by a strong commitment to your organization. You remember the gift plans that came together easily, with everyone working in harmony. You wince when you recall the plans plagued with problems from the beginning.

You have stories that inspire a smile and tales that make you sad. You recall voices, faces and places. You taste those cookies and that cup of coffee at a kitchen table. You remember one donor's trepidation, another's exuberance.

Your life as a gift planner is unique. No one else has your blend of experiences and insights. You are special! You could write a book!

Well, why not? At least, why not begin a daily or weekly journal of your experiences, insights and reflections. You could title it: "On My Way in Planned Giving."

Bulk Copies

On My Way in Planned Giving may be ordered in bulk for distribution to staff members, board members and other interested groups. For special discounted rates, contact the publisher at:

Planned Giving Today
2315 NW 198th Street
Seattle WA 98177
1-800-KALL-PGT